The Eighth Day

Letters, Poems and Parables
by Chuck Meyer

ISBN #09631149-1-3 $8.95

For Debi and Michal who help me live in the Eighth Day now, and for Deb, Uncle Carl and "Mom," who unknowingly told me how to get there.

CONTENTS

FOREWORD   vii

THE EIGHTH DAY   4

THE PARALYTIC'S POINT OF VIEW   11

TOMMY   18

TWO PARTS OF THE SAME PERSON CONVERSING
AT THE FEEDING OF THE 5000   28

AMOS, ZEB AND THE COLT   35

QUICKENING   43

THE AGATHON SCROLL   49

SYDNEY AND MORTIMER IN HELL   54

LETTER FROM MIRIAM   63

PRISONERS OF HOPE   74

HEART MURMURS   81

THREE DAY'S IN SAUL'S HEAD   88

MS. WIZ   97

PALM READER   108

LETTER FROM PRISON   118

A MAN'S BEST FRIEND IS HIS DEMON   125

LEPER LETTER   136

LETTER FROM NAIN   147

THE LAWYER'S CONFESSION   154

THE WIDOW'S STORY   163

REFERENCES   174

FOREWORD

The Eighth Day is the day after God finished making everything and rested. It is the time *after* the seventh day and *before* Jesus comes back. It is the arena of the moving of the Holy Spirit. It is a time of laughter, play, birth, death, sadness, stillness, dance, music, noise, dialogue, sickness, war, absurdity, questions, healing, giving, and peace. It is a time of being. It is sort of a Christian Twilight Zone where the Holy Spirit plays Rod Serling.

The stories included here are written in and for The Eighth Day. They have a different slant on the Bible and on God. They read the Gospel through different glasses. They see and celebrate the ordinariness of God and Christ Jesus and the people with whom they interact. Therefore, they have taken ordinary forms: letters, poetry, dialogues, stories about seemingly minor characters in the familiar Bible stories we all know.

For some, the stories will be confrontive, for others comforting - just like the Gospel. For everyone, I hope, they will be entertaining and challenging.

This collection is dedicated to my wife Debi and our ten year old daughter Michal, because many of the stories sound amazingly similar to the conversations we have around our rather silly house, and because my Eighth Day life with them is rich in indelible images and equally indelible love.

The other people in the dedication also have their stories. Deb, my first wife, who died in 1982, supported and critiqued the theology presented here, along with the literary style and accuracy of ideas. Further back, my Uncle Carl pitched a fit after every Sunday service because the preaching in the Episcopal Church of my childhood was never Biblical enough for him. I am certain that I was urged (or commanded) to see the Gospel in a different way by listening to him hold forth for years at the Sunday Germanic family get togethers amidst smoke, pinochle and beer. He especially would like these. Finally - furthest back - are the memories of my grandmother who everybody from the family to the neighbors called "Mom". She would rock me on our front porch and tell me made-up stories for what seemed like hours; stories that had drama, heroes and villains, laughter and tears, told in the safety of her soft lap and certain hands — just like the Gospel. She would like these too, and I believe she will somehow get to hear them.

Finally, I am also grateful for the regular attenders of the five o'clock service at St. David's Episcopal Church in Austin, Texas, for their responsiveness, encouragement, and support. It was there that most of these stories were first told.

As they are read and experienced, may these re-
flections on The Eighth Day call forth the kingdom in
us all, and may that kingdom be a surprising one of
peace that passes all understanding.

Austin, Texas
November, 1991

Genesis 1.1-2, 2

In the beginning God created the heavens and the earth. The earth was without form and void, and darkness was upon the face of the deep; and the Spirit of God was moving over the face of the waters. And God said, "Let there be light" and there was light. And God saw that the light was good; and God separated the light from the darkness. God called the light Day, and the darkness he called Night. And there was evening and there was morning, one day.

And God said, "Let there be a firmament in the midst of the waters, and let it separate the waters from the waters." And God made the firmament and separated the waters which were under the firmament from the waters which were above the firmament. And it was so. And God called the firmament Heaven. And there was evening and there was morning, a second day.

And God said, "Let the waters under the heavens be gathered together into one place, and let the dry land appear." And it was so. God called the dry land Earth, and the waters that were gathered together he called Seas. And God saw that it was good. And God said, "Let the earth put forth vegetation, plants yielding seed, and fruit trees bearing fruit in which is their seed, each according to its kind, upon the earth." And it was so. The earth brought forth vegetation, plants yielding seed according to their own kinds, and trees bearing fruit in which is their seed, each according to its kind. And God saw that it was good. And there was evening and there was morning, a third day.

And God said, "Let there be lights in the firmament of the heavens to separate the day from the night; and let them be for signs and for seasons and for days and years, and let them be lights in the firmament of the heavens to give light upon the earth." And it was so. And God made the two great lights, the greater light to rule the day, and the lesser light to rule the night; he made the stars also. And God set them in the firmament of the heavens to give light upon the earth, to rule over the day and over the night, and to separate the light from the darkness. And God saw that it was good. And there was evening and there was morning, a fourth day.

And God said, "Let the waters bring forth swarms of living creatures, and let birds fly above the earth across the firmament of the heavens." So God created the great sea monsters and every living creature that moves, with which the waters swarm, according to their kinds, and every winged bird according to its kind. And God saw that it was good. And God blessed them, saying, "Be fruitful and multiply and fill the waters in the seas, and let birds multiply on the earth." And there was evening and there was morning, a fifth day.

And God said, "Let the earth bring forth living creatures according to their kinds: cattle and creeping things and beasts of the earth according to their kinds." And it was so. And God made the beasts of the earth according to their kinds and the cattle according to their kinds, and everything that creeps upon the ground according to its kind. And God saw that it was good.

Then God said, "Let us make man in our image, after our likeness; and let them have dominion over the fish of the sea, and over the birds of the air, and over the cattle, and over all the earth, and over every creeping thing that creeps upon the earth." So God created man in his own image, in the image of God he created him;

male and female he created them. And God blessed them, and God said to them, "Be fruitful and multiply, and fill the earth and subdue it; and have dominion over the fish of the sea and over the birds of the air and over every living thing that moves upon the earth." And God said, "Behold, I have given you every plant yielding seed which is upon the face of all the earth, and every tree with seed in its fruit; you shall have them for food. And to every beast of the earth, and to every bird of the air, and to everything that creeps on the earth, everything that has the breath of life, I have given every green plant for food." And God saw everything that he had made, and behold, it was very good. And there was evening and there was morning, a sixth day.

Thus the heavens and the earth were finished, and all the host of them. And on the seventh day God finished his work which he had done. So God blessed the seventh day and hallowed it, because on it God rested from all his work which he had done in creation.

THE EIGHTH DAY

On the eighth day
God got up from his sabbatical
and stretched his Iberian body long and tall.
He looked out over the heavens and watched
through dusky eyes
the rising, gentle rising of the newmorning sun.
He rubbed his eyes and yawned the yawn of a man
    sore from
his labours, whose muscles ached with memories proud
of work well done.
God breathed
and with his breath all life breathed with him
and God smelled the freshness of his crisp day
and God felt the coolness of the breeze forming tiny
water droplets on the hair of his forearms.
God saw the fading stars of morning, the translucent
    wafer moon
and the disappearing darkness.
Then slowly, slowly as the sunrise, God's ancient teeth
    showed through
his bearded mouth and God smiled and thought

"Yes."

Some noise it must have been then that caught God's
   attention
for, still smiling, he looked down
and saw the first day firmament
subdivided, sold, sewn with chemicals, fertilized,
   ashpaltized
to quickly cover its new nakedness.
He saw the second day waters claimed and named,
   locked and damned and
dying; rivers fouled and acid rains and drought drenching
   former forests
God blinked and caught a glimpse of third day vegetation
   being hoarded
and used as weapons to claim more firmament for the
   few. He saw
defoliation and genetic standardization
saw strange colors and heard strange tastes
and lusting for his competition-god
Consumption.
The fourth day lights were somewhat still intact except
   for the one with
metal junk and forever footprints.
New lights he found fascinating, flashing neon nonsense
   to the nameless
passing numbers, praying
preying them to come consume.
Birds and fifth day fish floated past God's purview,
   proving it hard to
fly in air you could see and to swim in water you
   couldn't.
Sixth day beasts searched for safety from cement ribbons
while their cattle counterparts, their necks in stocks,
   were

forcefed, fattening faster for the tables of those trying to
     succeed.
God then looked down, furtherdown, down to the
     nethermost parts of his
creation and saw
grinning
man and woman
who looked back at him and shouted
"You said 'subdue' didn't you?"
"How sad," thought God, "how mad and bad their
     Hebrew is, I meant
'to cherish.'"
Then God closed his burning eyes
and said
nothing.

About the third hour
of the eighth day
God felt the strange sensation of another hand
taking his and firmly grasping
palm to calloused palm
while another gently laid on top.
God's heavy eyelids slowly opened
to find a sun of a different color
Jesus
there before him.
"Daddy," Jesus said
as he had said so many times before,
"I have been with them
and I have been them
and I am them.
I have grinned
and I have felt the rush of power
overwhelming and so tempting
to the taste of those who feel
so empty and alone."

"Do they not hear?"
God asked.
"Do they not hear, and see and feel and taste and touch
    and think
as we whose breath they carry?"
"Of course they do," said Jesus,
his almond eyes squinting and his saffron skin gleaming
in the nearly noonday sun,
"...that is their problem and their pain and their beauty.
They know our presence/breath and they know their
human finite endingness
and they are rest-less in the constant choosing."
God's broad brow wrinkled.
"But I thought," he said quite quietly
"that you and all the others,
you especially,
had shown them the Way."
"I did," Jesus replied,
"and still I understand their search for
more than human-ness
although it always ends in less than
human-ness."
Then Jesus took God's other hand in his
yellow brown yellow brown
and said
"Daddy, forgive them for they know not what they do."
"That is not true," God said, releasing his son's hands.
"They know exactly what they're doing."
And there was silence over God's being
from the sixth to the ninth hour.

At the eleventh hour
There shuffled across heaven
in worn down faded mules
a rotund black being with bloodshot eyes

7

surrounding deep ebony irises.
"How are y'all today?" she asked through gleaming
    teeth,
one gold one right in front.
And God replied,
"I'm glad that you are here."
"Me too," she said, "me, too.
Been plowin' fertile fields all day
a-sewin' and a-plantin' and a-movin' in and out and
all around our first day firmament
through waters, beasts and cattle and..."
(she raised her amber palm and looked up skyward)
"yes, Lord, my God even through our man and woman."
"Perhaps then you can tell us
Holy Spirit
why it is that they won't let us love them?"
"Yes," she smiled and slapped her hand upon her
meaty thigh.
"Yes sweet Jesus I can tell y'all that.
It is because they fear our mercy
more then they do our anger."
"I understand," said Jesus.
"Mercy is so undeserved and yet so freeing
that to say one is forgiven
means a cleansing and renewing
that looks frightening when compared with what they
    know."
The Holy Spirit moved her bulk
to table where three chairs sat
and said
"Come let's eat and drink together
bread and wine and watch creation
one through seven
re-create itself
now with our help."
God and Jesus joined her.

Then God got up and fetched
a fourth chair,
setting it at table with them.
"We got comp'ny comin' Lawd o' mercy?"
Holy Spirit smiled and stuffed
her wiry hair up under her bandanna.
"That," said God
now sitting, elbows on the table,
fingers interlaced
"...that is my deepest hope."
"Perhaps," said Jesus
taking each one's hand in his
"it is enough
to know the invitation's open
and the chair is
free."

The conversation mellowed
as the sun sank into darkness.
There was evening.
There was morning.
And the eighth day
was done.

Mark 2.1-12

And when he returned to Capernaum after some days, it was reported that he was at home. And many were gathered together, so that there was no longer room for them, not even about the door; and he was preaching the word to them. And they came, bringing to him a paralytic carried by four men. And when they could not get near him because of the crowd, they removed the roof above him; and when they had made an opening they let down the pallet on which the paralytic lay. And when Jesus saw their faith, he said to the paralytic, "My son, your sins are forgiven."

Now some of the scribes were sitting there, questioning in their hearts, "Why does this man speak thus:? It is blasphemy! Who can forgive sins but God alone:? And immediately Jesus, perceiving in his spirit that they thus questioned within themselves, said to them, "Why do you question thus in your hearts? Which is easier, to say to the paralytic, 'Your sins are forgiven,' or to say 'Rise, take up your pallet and walk'? But that you may know that the Son of man has authority on earth to forgive sins" - he said to the paralytic - "I say to you, rise, take up your pallet and go home." And he rose, and immediately took up the pallet and went out before them all; so that they were all amazed and glorified God, saying, "We never saw anything like this!"

The Paralytic's Point of View

I feel lousy. It is another day. Maybe *this* will be the day I die. I can't talk. I can't move. I blink my eyes. I eat. I sleep. I take that back. I do not eat. I am fed. I do not sleep. I am put to bed. I am an object for others to tend. They watch me. They clean up after me. They wish the same wishes I wish, though we do not tell each other. We are not supposed to wish death, you know. We are supposed to figure out what God is doing in our lives.

God knows how I feel. I have told him enough in no uncertain terms. I resent living like this. I resent existing like this. I watch the sun come up and cannot tell anyone else of its horrible beauty. It is overwhelmingly beautiful to me - and it is horrible because it means another day that I cannot move.

And so I lie here, watching the day pass through this town of Capernaum, unable to scratch my bleeding bedsores, unable to swish the fly from my cheek, unable to tell my family I love them. They do not deserve me, my family. It has been so long. I cannot now remember when I was not paralyzed. I think it must have been...

What is that noise? This is usually a quiet neighborhood. I hope it is not the soldiers again, or those rowdies who come through and make trouble. What? What are they doing coming in here? My friends - four of them - what are you doing? You are covering me with a blanket. You are lifting up my pallet and taking me outside. This must be something to see!

What is it? What are you taking me to see? A traveling caravan? A new sorcerer? Hey, be careful you dolt! Don't drop me! Easy now. Set me down easy. That's it. Well, what is it? All I see is a commotion and lots of people crowding into the house over there. What are you thinking? Why won't you talk to me? What are you huddling up and talking about among yourselves?

Hey! Don't leave me here! Hey ! That's not nice - you drag me out of my own house and leave me here lying in the middle of the dusty street while you run off and....what are you doing with that ladder? Oh, if I could only talk! Why won't you talk to me? Tell me what you're doing!

We'll never get near that house. There are too many peop....Oh Lord...are you ever in trouble now! You can't do that! Get down off that roof! I've never seen you like this. You are my friends. We have quiet drinks together. You sit and tell me the latest stories and jokes. You read me from Torah and tell me I'll get better. You are my normal, everyday friends. What's gotten in to you? Why are you tearing that man's roof apart?

Good heavens that's a big hole. Why you could almost...Oh no..that's enough! Take me back! Put me down! Don't lift me up that ladder! I know you've strapped me on with tight rope, but I'm so hard to maneuver! What are you doing? You're going to drop me! I'm scared! I don't want to hurt any more than I do! Let me down! Get me off this roof! I'm frightened!

Now what are you doing? What are those ropes for? Oh no. Don't *do* that! Don't lower me down...who is this man anyway? Who asked you to get involved in my life? I'm so embarrassed. Look at all those people. I'm scared! I'm angry! Be careful!

That's strange. The man in the center of the room. He is not looking at *me* - he's staring at *you*. And he's smiling! He's standing over me and helping you lower me to the floor. He's kneeling beside me and taking my hand in his. What hands! He's talking. What's that? I can hardly hear the words because of the crowd. I'm squinting at them to tell him to repeat it. He understands! He's saying it again, closer to me now. "My...son...your...sins...are forgiven...."

That's incredible! It's so simple. I feel strange. I feel relaxed. I feel accepted as never before. I feel intimately involved with this man even though we're here in front of lots of people. I feel as though my tightness and paralysis are draining from me. I feel...wait a minute... What are those scribes saying? I am distracted from this man. They are making so much noise. They are saying it is blasphemy! They are telling him only God can forgive sins. Maybe they're right. Maybe I should listen to them. Maybe...oh...no...I feel tighter and more paralyzed again.

What's this man saying now? He's talking back to them and asking them a question. I like his voice. He speaks with authority. His voice and manner are comforting to me. Here he comes again - he's speaking to me again. He's saying...what's that...I don't believe it! He's saying "Rise, take up your pallet and go home."

Doesn't he understand! Doesn't he know I can't move? Doesn't he respect my illness? Doesn't he respect my paralysis? Doesn't he see what everyone else sees — that I am paralyzed, that I am useless, that I am...no, he sees none of those things. He seems to see something else.

How I wish I could see it too. Oh, God, I don't know who to listen to. Should I listen to this man who tells me to be more than I am now? Should I keep in my religious tradition and listen to my religious people and be conservative and rigid and pious and godly? And what if I do listen to him? What kind of life will I have? I will have to have full responsibility for myself, for my actions, my words, my behavior. I have grown to almost *like* my paralysis - no, that is not the word. But perhaps it is that I *know* my paralysis - yes, that *is* the word, I am more comfortable with *it* than I am with the unknown that awaits me if I listen to this man. He is waiting for an answer.

I have made my decision. And my decision is not just an intellectual one. He won't settle for that. My decision has to be shown in my behavior. And so it will.

I feel warmth now spreading over my body. I feel strength ebbing into places it has never been before. I feel life pulsating through my limbs. I am moving my legs. I am moving my arms. I am sitting. I am slowly standing. I reach down and pick up my pallet and walk through the pathway made by the stunned crowd and the angry scribes.

I am out of the house and standing alone now in the street. The pallet I carry is a reminder of where I came from. It is important that I did not leave it with that man. It was not his pallet to carry for me. It is mine to carry with my own strength. I am responsible for what I do with this, my former infirmity.

What's that shouting? I run around and see my friends on the roof shouting and waving at me. I wave back - a slow, grateful wave.

Through the crowd I see the man in the center of the house. Someone else is standing in front of him now and he is laying his hands on him. The scribes are still screaming at him. And he is answering them back. He briefly glances out at me.

I mouth the words - the first words I have said, actually said, in years. My mouth is so dry. The words feel strange. Tears wet my parched lips. The air passes up through unused vocal cords and over a thick tongue. The sound, barely audible, is formed with lips unused to moving.

His eyes meet mine and he smiles as he watches my mouth say the scratchy words - "Thank You."

John 6.3-15

Now the Passover, the feast of the Jews, was at hand. Lifting up his eyes, then, and seeing that a multitude was coming to him, Jesus said to Philip, "How are we to buy bread, so that these people may eat?" This he said to test him, for he himself knew what he would to. Philip answered him, "Two hundred denarii would not buy enough bread for each of them to get a little."

One of his disciples, Andrew, Simon Peter's brother, said to him, "There is a lad here who has five barley loaves and two fish; but what are they among so many?" Jesus said, "Make the people sit down."

Now there was much grass in the place; so the men sat down, in number about five thousand. Jesus then took the loaves, and when he had given thanks, he distributed them to those who were seated; so also the fish, as much as they wanted.

And when they had eaten their fill, he told his disciples, "Gather up the fragments left over, that nothing may be lost." So they gathered them up and filled twelve baskets with fragments from the five barley loves, left by those who had eaten. When the people saw the sign which he had done, they said, "This is indeed the prophet who is to come into the world!"

Tommy

Nine year old Tommy slowly walked down the dusty road, kicking at stones and clods of dirt with his sandal.

"She's gonna kill me, I know she's gonna kill me," he thought dejectedly.

He looked down at the basket he was carrying. Where once there had been five beautiful loaves and two fish, now there were only lots of crumbs, hunks of bread torn off and replaced, bits of grass in among them, gathered by that prophet's disciples, handled by that whole crowd of people.

"Holy Moses! I know she's gonna kill me. I tried to convince her I was old enough to go to the market and bring home the stuff she wanted. I put the money in my pocket and held it there all the way into town. I kept the towel over the basket all the way so no dust would get in. I went to the people in the market Momma always goes to when I'm with her. I took lots of time to pick out just the right fish and the prettiest barley loaves so she'd be proud of me - so she'd know I was big enough to help her."

He stopped long enough to pick up a stone and hurl it, hard as he could, at a crow sitting on a fence post. The stone hit the post and the bird, squawking its contempt, flapped excitedly away.

"Stupid bird," Tommy thought. "Stupid bird? Stupid ME! How could I have ever offered that man our family's dinner? What got into me? What was his name? Jesus something or other? It was like I was in a dream. Maybe that's it - maybe this is all a dream and I'll wake up soon and..."

He again looked down at the crumb filled basket, and he looked up ahead at the front door of his house.

"This is no dream," he thought. "This is a nightmare! Okay - in a minute I'm going to go knock on that door and tell Momma the absolute truth. I'm gonna tell her exactly what happened. I'm gonna say: `Momma, I did just like you said. I went straight into town, bought the loaves and fish and headed home. Then you'll never guess what happened! A forty foot giant with two heads and six eyes jumped out from behind a bush and ate the fish and tore up all the bread. I was lucky to escape with this basket of crumbs!'"

He stood before the door to his house, about to knock. "Nope, she'll never buy that one. Besides I used it once before and..."

The door opened and Tommy's mother bent down to hug her son.

"Tommy! I was getting worried about you! What took you so long? I'm glad you made it home safely, though. I guess I was wrong about you. You certainly are turning into a young man faster than I thought. You went all the way into town and back and..."

Tommy's eyes started to water. He felt a big lump form in his throat and the edges of his small mouth began to draw down.

"Momma....Momma, I didn't...I couldn't....I...."

He dissolved into tears as his mother hugged him close. With her free hand she lifted the towel to see the pile of bread crumbs. Rolling her eyes to the heavens she thought: "Master of the Universe, I asked you to look over him - and now what has happened?"

Tommy regained his composure for a moment.

"I'm sorry, Momma. I really am! I really did it right. I kept close hold on the money and I didn't dawdle - well not too much anyway - and I bought the best loaves and the prettiest fish."

"And then what did you do, Tommy?" She held him at arm's length.

"I was coming through one of the hills on the way home and there were all these people gathered, listening to some man. I think he was a prophet or something. That's what some of the people whispered while he talked. I figured I could sit and rest a while and still get home pretty quick, so I did."

Tommy's eyes lit up.

"Oh, Momma! You should have heard him! There were lots and lots of people there and he had them all spellbound - and me too. He was wonderful, Momma. He spoke about freedom and love and justice and peace."

"Tommy, Tommy, Tommy." His mother gently smoothed the hair on his head. "You've heard those people before. They're a denarius a dozen. They're always attracting a crowd for a short time and then they vanish into the wind."

"Not this one, Momma. He was different. He talked about those things as though he really meant them. And he told us - could I have a glass of water, Momma?"

Tommy's mother brought in a clay cup with fresh well water. Then, between gulps, Tommy explained.

"He told us that WE were the ones who controlled all those things. It wasn't hard even for *me* to understand. He made it so simple."

"So what about our dinner?"

"That's the weird part, Momma. People had been there a while and everyone wanted something to eat. I was the only one with food but I knew it wouldn't feed all those people. I thought it would feed him though, so I said, 'Here, mister, take this for yourself and your friends.' I couldn't help it Momma. I just couldn't stop myself. Around that man I just wanted to give everything I had."

"And what happened when your little basket didn't go very far?"

"That's just it, Momma." Tommy got excited as he talked. "That's just it! That Jesus person said a blessing over it and - Momma you're not gonna believe this..."

(he closed his eyes and shrunk down small) "...everybody got fed and they took up 12 baskets of leftovers."

Tommy's mother looked at him closely. If he was lying she would whack the daylights out of him. If he was telling the truth he had been blessed with witnessing the presence of a true prophet of God.

She decided Tommy was not lying. He was a lot more confident when he lied.

Tommy squinted one eye open, waiting for the blow. "Are you gonna hit me, Momma?"

"No, Tommy. I'm not."

"You're not?" He opened the other eye and smiled.

"No. Sometimes these things happen."

Tommy looked at her suspiciously. She had never been this understanding before.

"Sometimes WHAT things happen, Momma?"

She took his hand and looked at him intently.

"Sometimes, Tommy, when our baskets are full we become so overwhelmed at God's presence in our lives and at the abundance He provides us that we want to give it back to him. Just like this Jesus you saw, God is attractive like that. The ironic thing is that, instead of keeping it for himself, he gives it away to others who need it.

"Also when we give something to God and He blesses it, it becomes much more than it was when we so tightly held onto it. It multiplies, goes farther, sometimes even changes form and meaning. Do you understand, Tommy?"

"I think I do, Momma."

"Then you truly are a young man, Tommy. One more question, though."

"What's that, Momma?"

"What happened to this prophet you saw?"

"Well, when I left, people were shouting after him that he was 'indeed the prophet who is to come into the world!' And some said they wanted to take him by force and make him king. Last I saw he was heading into the hills to get away from them."

"Master of the Universe," she thought. "I wonder if it is The Anointed One?" Her thoughts were interrupted by her son.

"Momma, what're we gonna do about dinner tonight? Papa and the rest of the kids will be in from the fields any minute now and they're not gonna be real happy about what happened."

"Don't worry, Tommy. We'll find something here. In fact we..."

There was a knock at the door.

"Who's that?" Tommy asked.

There was another knock.

"Can't be opportunity," his mother said, "it only knocks once."

"What?"

"Never mind."

She opened the door to find a tall, bearded man holding a basket covered with a cloth.

"Does a lad named 'Tommy' live here?" he asked.

"Yes, but who are you?"

Tommy ran to the door. "It's him, Momma! It's him!"

"The prophet?"

"No. One of his friends! I don't know his name. He's the one I gave the basket to!"

"My name is Andrew," the man said. "My brother is a fisherman. His name is Peter. We both met your son just outside of town where our teacher was talking to the people. Your son, in his generosity, gave us all that he had. That is more than most people give in their entire lifetimes, I can assure you.

"Yes. We were just talking about it," Tommy's mother said.

"I hope you weren't too hard on him," Andrew said.

"She wasn't hard at all, Mr. Andrew, sir. She said she understood that sometimes these things happen."

"You are blessed to have such understanding with each other. That was the concern of our master, Jesus. He has a special place in his heart for children — says you can't understand God if you're not like a child — and he also remembered when he got into trouble with his parents when he was about Tommy's age. He had us ask around to find out where you lived. Then Simon Peter, my brother, brought some of the abundant catch he'd gotten this afternoon to me and asked me to find you."

Andrew handed Tommy the basket. Tommy took the cloth off and found six beautiful fish and nine fresh barley loaves.

"Momma, LOOK!! Look at all the food!" Tommy was wide-eyed.

"Are you sure you can spare these, Andrew?" his mother asked.

"Yes, we're sure. And Jesus sends his blessing and his love to Tommy and to his family."

"Then be sure to thank him for us. He is most generous. We will accept his gift to us."

"I will tell him. And yes, he is generous. Maybe that's why Tommy found it so easy to give to him. They must be alot alike."

Andrew turned to leave.

"Good bye now," he said.

"Good bye Mr. Andrew, sir!" Tommy yelled.

"Good bye," his mother whispered.

Later that night the family sat around the wooden dinner table feasting on bread, wine and broiled fish together. The main topic of conversation was, of course, Tommy and all he had witnessed that day.

"You know, Tommy," his mother said, "when you first started to explain what happened I thought for sure you were going to tell me some story about a forty foot giant with six eyes and two heads."

"Who, ME?" Tommy grinned as he broke off another piece of the barley loaf. "Never in a million years!"

Mark 6.30-34

The apostles returned to Jesus, and told him all that they had done and taught. And he said to them, "Come away by yourselves to a lonely place, and rest a while." For many were coming and going, and they had no leisure even to eat. And they went away in the boat to a lonely place by themselves.

Now many saw them going, and knew them, and they ran there on foot from all the towns, and got there ahead of them. As he landed he saw a great throng, and he had compassion on them, because they were like sheep without a shepherd; and he began to teach them many things. And when it grew late, his disciples came to him and said, "This is a lonely place, and the hour is now late; send them away, to go into the country and villages round about and buy themselves something to eat." But he answered them, "You give them something to eat."

And they said to him, "Shall we go and buy two hundred denarii worth of bread, and give it to them to eat?"

And he said to them "How many loaves have you? Go and see." And when they had found out, they said, "Five, and two fish." Then he commanded them all to sit down by companies upon the green grass. So they sat down in groups, by hundreds and by fifties. And taking the five loaves and the two fish he looked up to heaven, and blessed, and broke the loaves, and gave them to the disciples to set before the people; and he divided the two fish among them all.

And they all ate and were satisfied. And they took up twelve baskets full of broken pieces and of the fish. And those who ate the loaves were five thousand men.

Two Parts of the Same Person Conversing at the Feeding of the 5000

(The two parts stand with their backs to each other, facing away.)

(1) The two of us, myself

(2) And I

(1) Have followed him

(2) This Jesus person is who he means

(1) I

(2) He and I

(1) Have followed Jesus the entire day

(2) The whole week he means

(1) And now it's late and I am hungry

(2) You're always hungry. That's all you think about is food.

(1) And we're out here in this lonely place.

(2) Not a Taco Bell in sight.

(1) I feel lonely and it's late.

(2) How can you feel lonely with 5000 people?

(1) I've had lots of practice. Aren't you lonely?

(2) I'm too angry to be lonely.

(1) That's the reason I don't like you.

(2) I don't like you either.

(1) We're so different, you and I.

(2) You always do things wrong.

(1) You seldom do things right.

(2) You're selfish.

(1) You're arrogant.

(2) You're frightened.

(1) You're lustful.

(2) I have more fun than you do.

(1) I get more done than you do.

(2) That's what you think.

(1) Wait a minute!

(2) Don't stop now! We've been doing this a long time.

(1) All our lives.

(2) So what? The whole world does it.

(1) Calls names.

(2) Argues.

(1) Fights about colors.

(2) And possessions.

(1) And beliefs in God.

(2) The world is divided.

(1) Just like we are.

(2) Hey! Look up there!

(1 and 2 turn slightly toward the front of the crowd.)

(1) What's going on?

(2) They're arguing.

(1) Jesus and his disciples are arguing.

(2) They're divided too.

(1) What are they saying?

(2) Who cares?

(1) Something about food.

(2) Your hearing improves when people mention food.

(1) One of them wants to send us away.

(2) Great. Drag us all out here and starve us to death. Typical prophet.

(1) All you do is complain.

(2) All you do is comply.

(1) You're hostile.

(2) You're passive.

(1) Jesus!

(2) Don't swear.

(1) I mean Jesus is talking.

(2) Big deal.

(1) He's telling his friends to feed us.

(2) From that bunch we'll probably get bread crumbs.

(1) He's holding up some loaves.

(2) And a fish in each hand.

(1) Holy Mackerel!

(2) That's not funny.

(1) I mean there's suddenly all this food.

(2) I wonder if it's safe to eat it?

(1) You're so cynical.

(2) You're so gullible.

(1) What could possibly happen?

(2) Maybe it's a trick.

(1) Jesus wouldn't trick us.

(2) I don't trust him.

(1) I don't trust you.

(2) That's what I fear.

(1) You fear me?

(2) No. I fear that if we eat this meal together...

(1) Yes, go on.

(2) ....we might stop fighting.

(1) Good heavens! Now I'm scared too!

(2) What would we do if we didn't argue?

(1) How would we act if we weren't hostile?

(2) Who would believe us?

(1) It's quite a risk.

(2) I don't know if I want to change.

(1) I'm not sure I do either.

(2) They're passing around the bread.

(1) They're passing around the fish.

(2) We have to decide.

(1) It's now or never.

(2) (slowly) I'm so hungry.

(1) (slowly) I'm so hungry.

(2) Let's

(1) eat.

    (1 and 2 slowly turn to face each other.)

(2) I feel strange.

(1) So do I.

(2) Here, let me feed you.

(1) Thanks. Now let me feed you.

(2) Thanks. What are you staring at?

(1) You. Me. Us. We. It's like I've never seen you this way.

(2) I see you also in a new way.

(1) I have something to say.

(2) I do too.

(1) I forgive you.

(2) I forgive you.

(1) I wonder what

(2) was in that bread?

(1) Probably the

(2) Holy Spirit.

(1) I feel

(2) satisfied now.

(1) And

(2) full. Quite

(1) full.

(2) You know

(1) what this means,

(2) don't you?

(1) Yes. It means after

(2) all this time

(1) we're One.

(2) We're One.

   (1 and 2 turn to face the crowd.)

(1) & (2) One.

(1) & (2) I want to go thank Jesus for spiking the bread and fish.

(1) & (2) I wonder what they'll do with the leftovers?

(1) & (2) Maybe they'll hand them out to all these people here, that we may all - ALL - all parts of ourselves, all parts of the church, all parts of the world, that we may all be one.

(1) & (2) One.

(1) & (2) Amen.

Mark 11.1-11

And when they drew near to Jerusalem, to Bethphage and Bethany, at the Mount of Olives, he sent two of his disciples, and said to them, "Go into the village opposite you, and immediately as you enter it you will find a colt tied, on which no one has ever sat; untie it and bring it. If any one says to you, 'Why are you doing this?' say, 'The Lord has need of it and will send it back here immediately.'"

And they went away, and found a colt tied at the door out in the open street; and they untied it. And those who stood there said to them, "What are you doing, untying the colt?" And they told them what Jesus had said; and they let them go.

And they brought the colt to Jesus, and threw their garments on it; and he sat upon it. And many spread their garments on the road, and others spread leafy branches which they had cut from the fields. And those who went before and those who followed cried out, "Hosanna! Blessed is he who comes in the name of the Lord! Blessed is the kingdom of our father David that is coming! Hosanna in the highest."

And he entered Jerusalem, and went into the temple; and when he had looked round at everything, as it was already late, he went out to Bethany with the twelve.

Amos, Zeb and the Colt

Amos and Zebulon leaned lazily against the wooden doorway where the colt was tied. Amos, short as his name, rubbed his stubby hand over the two day growth of whiskers on his face, thinking. Zebulon, tall and thin as a cedar post, reached his long arm into the back pocket of his faded frayed jeans and pulled out the rumpled packet of Red Man. Opening it, he first offered the sweet smelling laces of tobacco to his friend. Amos shook his head, still thinking.

Zebulon chewed. Amos rubbed. They both stared at the colt. Finally Amos spoke:

"That sure is a mighty fine colt." he pronounced.

"Yup." Zebulon answered. "It shore is."

"Ain't yet a yearling, is he, Zeb?"

"Nope. 'Bout a month shy."

"Sure is a purty color."

"Yup." Zebulon said as he spit into the dusty road. "Part Arabian."

"Shore am glad we bought him, Zeb."

"Yup. Me too."

Amos looked over at his friend. "What we gonna do with him?"

Zebulon glanced sideways through the slits that were his eyes. "Reckon we're gonna ride him, dontcha think?"

They both looked at the colt, who seemed to understand their intentions. Amos rubbed. Zebulon chewed. The colt snorted.

"Ain't been rode yet, has he, Zeb?"

"Nope. Not even saddled."

Amos thought a minute. "Who's gonna ride him first, Zeb?"

Zebulon spoke softly. "You are."

Amos stopped rubbing. He was about to speak when two strangers coming down the road caught his attention.

"Those fellas shore are walkin' in a hurry," he said. "Looks like they're comin' this way."

Zebulon aimed at a bug on the ground. "Yup."

As the two approached, Amos, without moving from his spot, began: "Howdy, gents. What you fellas want?"

The two strangers began to untie the thick tether from the doorpost. Without looking at either Zebulon or Amos, one of the strangers replied: "This colt."

Zebulon reached out a lanky arm and grabbed the man by the shoulder.

"What're you boys doin', untyin' that colt? Aintcha got no manners? That there colt belongs to *us*."

The strangers looked at the two men. One of them spoke: "The Lord needs it, and will send it back here immediately."

Zebulon released the stranger's shoulder from his heavy grip. "Whyncha say so?" he said, distributing more tobacco juice evenly into the dust.

The strangers, without further words, led the colt away and eventually out of sight.

Amos rubbed. Zebulon chewed.

Amos looked worriedly down the road. "The colt's gone, Zeb."

"Yup."

"Why'd you let them take him?"

"Why'd *you* let them take him?"

"Well, Zeb, I dunno. I sorta had this funny feelin' like we'd better."

"Yup."

Amos, pretending to understand, kept silent until he heard some commotion.

"Hey, lookit that, Zeb," he said. "Yonder comes our colt with some ol' boy ridin' him. And the colt ain't kickin' or fightin' or nothin'. Just swishin' his tail happy as you please."

Zebulon tipped up the brim of his Stetson and squinted his eyes almost shut. "Yup," he said. "What're all them people doin' throwin' down stuff in the road?"

"Looks like he's some kind of prophet or somethin'," Amos answered. "People are shoutin' 'Hosanna' and sayin' that he's bringin' in the kingdom of David."

Amos' eyes got big. He stood tall as he could, his

hands in his jeans pockets, staring at the approaching crowd. "You reckon, Zeb, this might be the fella people been talkin' about, this Jesus fella they been tellin' all the stories about?"

Zebulon stopped chewing, opened his squinting eyes a bit and said: "Yup. And he's ridin' *our* colt!"

As the crowd approached, Amos and Zebulon hurried over and met them with smiles.

"Hey, y'all," Zebulon said to no one in particular and to everyone he saw, "...that there's MY colt he's ridin'."

Amos argued back. "It's MY colt he's ridin'."

"MY colt!" Zebulon smiled and said, pointing to the man riding by.

"MY colt!" Amos pointed and smiled also, frowning when he heard Zebulon's voice.

They mingled in the crowd and watched as Jesus rode the colt the final hundred yards into the town. They proudly continued to proclaim their separate ownership of the fine animal and, hopefully, gained some association with the man riding him. They watched as Jesus dismounted from the colt and strode into the temple.

"Shore am glad I let them have that colt," Zebulon said, smiling.

"Shore am glad *I* let them have that colt," Amos said, smiling.

But his smile began to droop as he watched the tables being flung out the door of the temple. Feathers flew and coins dropped into the dust as Jesus threw the

birds and moneychangers out into the street. The crowd
began to look strangely at Amos and Zebulon.

"HIS colt!" Zebulon pointed at Amos.

"HIS colt!" Amos pointed at Zebulon.

"*You* said it was *yours*!"

"NO, *you* said it was *yours*!"

The crowd began to get unruly and the two men
fled as quickly as they could back to their small house.
They slammed the door shut, bolted it and stood with
their backs against it shaking in the darkened room.

Time passed. The noise died down. Evening came.
Amos and Zebulon still stood in the dark. Neither
spoke, until they heard the clip clop of hooves in the
dust.

The clip clopping stopped.

Amos, pushing Zebulon aside, carefully opened the
door just a crack and peeked out. There stood the colt
in the same place as before, its tether hanging down,
dragging on the ground.

"Well I'll be.....the colt's back, Zeb."

"Ain't nobody on him, is there?"

"No. Come on out. We need to tie him up to the
door again."

The colt was tied and the two men resumed their
former leaning positions.

Amos rubbed. Zebulon chewed. The colt swished.

"That's just like a prophet," Amos said after a while.

"Huh?" Zebulon mumbled.

"He gets people all fired up about bringing in the
kingdom and then goes and talks about stuff like feeding

the hungry and bein' with outcasts and overturnin' the tables of our religious system that works so well for us. No wonder people don't like him."

"Ain't his fault," Zebulon spit out.

"What?"

"I said, 'It ain't his fault.'" Zebulon drew a deep breath. "He just said he was bringin' in the kingdom. Didn't say nothin' about us likin' it or agreein' with it."

"Yeah, maybe, Zeb."

"Maybe nuthin'. Sometimes you gotta get your tables upset before you can see your way clear to do somethin' different."

Amos rubbed and said, "Zeb, how'd you get so wise all of a sudden?"

Zebulon aimed more juice into the darkness. "Been savin' it up a while," he said.

There was a long silence when each man seemed lost in thought. Then Amos stopped rubbing.

"That sure is a mighty fine colt," he pronounced.

"Yup," Zebulon answered. "It shore is."

"You s'pose that Jesus fella could use a coupla no-counts like us?"

"I dunno," Zebulon nearly whispered. "Risky."

"What you mean, 'Risky,' Zeb?"

"Mean it'd cost us a bunch, followin' that fella. More crowds. Doin' things people don't like. Goin' agin' our so-ciety, goin' agin' our comfortable friends."

Amos hesitated. "Maybe even goin' agin' our religion, Zeb?"

"Yup," Zebulon said in the darkness. "Risky," he repeated. "Risky."

Amos was quiet a minute, then said: "Be a good name for the colt, Zeb."

"What's that?"

"'Risky'," Amos ventured.

Zebulon's brown stained teeth showed in a smile. "Yup," he said. "And you know what else?"

"What, Zeb?"

"Followin' that Jesus fella, risky as it is, sure beats standin' here safe and bored."

"I bet he gets tired walkin' all the time," Amos said. "I bet he'd like to have this here colt to sit on now and then."

Zebulon looked through the darkness at Amos. "Let's see can we find him."

"Yeah," Amos smiled. "Let's."

They untied the tether and slowly ambled down the road in the intermittent moonlight. Amos rubbed. Zebulon chewed. Their conversation continued, backed by the syncopated counterpoint of the clip clop, clip clop of Risky.

Luke 9.18-24

Now it happened that as he was praying alone the disciples were with him; and he asked them, "Who do people say that I am?" And they answered, "John the Baptist; but others say, Elijah; and others, that one of the old prophets has risen."

And he said to them, "But who do you say that I am?" And Peter answered, "The Christ of God." But he charged and commanded them to tell this to no one saying: "The Son of man must suffer many things, and be rejected by the elders and chief priests and scribes, and be killed, and on the third day be raised."

And he said to all, "If any man would come after me, let him deny himself and take up his cross daily and follow me. For whoever would save his life will lose it; and whoever loses his life for my sake, he will save it.

QUICKENING

He sat at prayer, as was his custom
bearded chin in swollen calloused hand
legs crossed
eyes downward thinking
listening wondering hoping for an answer
to his constant question
from the One he thought would know.
No answer came.

He first sensed then heard then saw them
his disciples gently gathering always
following, wanting, asking,
Jesus tell us, help us, hold us
BE us Jesus since we can't be you.
He observed them sitting down before
him and he sighed deepsigh, painsigh
deathsigh.

Maybe they will know, he thought and
just before they started Jesus spoke

first saying
Who am I
to others?
Silence loud as daylight split
the air as once again
no answer came.
Slowly, one by one, some
raised their eyes and looking
at him said Depends
on who you ask
and when.

Ask a fisherman and you
are master of the catch or
some new Jonah prophet telling
us deeptruths of wind and water.
The physician wants you to be
healer of the suffering killer of the
hopeless comfort of the dead and
so you are.

For the revolutionary you
are revolution change rebellion
angerjustice seldompeace
confronting conscience of the
powerful who see you in what
ever way will help them keep
things as they are.

Jesus looking at each one
said sadly Tell me
Who am I
to you? and waited wanting
desperately to hear a word or

nod of knowing, knowing no one
would respond.

Silence stealthily surrounded them
as one man stood spoke slowly
Jesus staring shaking straining
not to hear the words he
feared were true.

Christ of God
said Peter galvanizing
all events and bringing whirlwind
history into perfect focus.
Christ of God
Jesus repeated words
indelible fell from his lips
incredible thoughts blurred his
racing mind incapable of comprehending
as his futurepast and present came
suddenly haltingly
too clear.

Movement stirred the group
with whispered glances secret
smiles cold terror trembling
side by side by side,
Finally Jesus stricken stood
embraced his friend held
him and being held by Peter softly
softly wept.

Minutes passed forever no
one moved or reached out
to him frightened by his

and their humanness.
Peter sitting Jesus turned
wiping his face upon his sleeve
and spoke
Tell no one of this.

Words you'll find are useless so
keep silent even to each other
rather go proclaim with
your own deeds go shout out
loud with your own actions
lose your life each day and
save it save
your life each day and lose
it matters to me which you choose to
do.

Murmuring they rose to leave
him standing Wait before you
go I want you each to ask yourself the
question I have asked of you Who
am I?

It is only when you lookdeep into
your own mirror that you see
me. It is only when you see me
clearly that you clearly
see yourself and others.
Who I am to you is who
you are to me is who
we are to God.

All had gone when Jesus
sat at prayer as was his custom

dusty beard in sweating hand
legs crossed
glazed eyes gazed outward
pondering wondering raging
Who am I
to
      me ?

And suddenly

    he

      knew.

John 2.1-11

On the third day there was a marriage at Cana in Galilee, and the mother of Jesus was there; Jesus also was invited to the marriage, with his disciples. When the wine failed, the mother of Jesus said to him, "They have no wine." And Jesus said to her, "O woman, what have you to do with me? My hour has not yet come." His mother said to the servants, "Do whatever he tells you."

Now six stone jars were standing there, for the Jewish rites of purification, each holding twenty or thirty gallons. Jesus said to them, "Fill the jars with water." And they filled them up to the brim. He said to them, "Now draw some out, and take it to the steward of the feast." So they took it.

When the steward of the feast tasted the water now become wine, and did not know where it came from (though the servants who had drawn the water knew), the steward of the feast called the bridegroom and said to him, "Every man serves the good wine first; and when men have drunk freely, then the poor wine; but you have kept the good wine until now." This, the first of his signs, Jesus did at Cana in Galilee, and manifested his glory; and his disciples believed in him.

THE AGATHON SCROLL

My name is Agathon the eunuch. I know that as a servant I should not write this, but what happened last night was so strange that I must set it down on this scroll; I must recount it to be sure it happened.

I was working my master's wedding here in Cana, Galilee. They are such a nice young couple, so caring with each other and so in love. I didn't even mind that some of their guests were rowdies. There was plenty to eat and drink and I was kept pretty busy refilling platters and jugs and cleaning up messes. None of the servants were too busy, though, to keep us from eating and drinking our share.

Actually I had drunk a little - let me be honest here - a LOT more than my share and had settled down in a comfortable corner to rest and have just one more goblet of that excellent Galilean red. As I watched the hurried movements of the other servants and listened to the din of the partying crowd my eyes became fixed on six large stone jars. They seemed to be the only things that weren't moving and proved restful for my spinning head.

The jars still had some water in them for purification rites rather than for drinking or even bathing. The more I stared at the jars the more everything else faded into a blur in the background. Then, and I swear this is what I experienced, it was as though I could hear the water speaking. Here is what it said:

I am water
I am lukewarm, impure, unfit
People see right through me
when the mud and debris settle
down enough. They use but
do not want me, pour me, spill me
for perfunctory prayers unthought of.
I sit here in stone jars
unattended unannounced unnoticed
waiting, always waiting wanting
always wanting to be wanted knowing
I will not be
ever anything but wasted unblessed
water I am
water I am
water.

I was in no mood for following her orders but I watched as my friends filled the stone jars the rest of the way up to the brim with more water. The guest, I think his name was Jesus, did something or other to the jars. I couldn't see because his back was to me. He then told another servant to take some of the liquid to the steward of the feast. We servants were the only ones that knew where it had come from and they didn't believe us at first when they found out the jars were now filled with a wonderful wine.

I stared at the jars again, and again I could swear this is what I heard:

I am wine
I am deep/rich and clear/red
People hold me want me give
me all their senses and desires
and I give them back in warm
and gentler tones.
I am well attended and attending
well announced announcing noticed
seldom waiting sought and used
to soften mingle gladden
never wasting in these stone jars
knowing now with His touch
His renaming
I am ever blessed and busy useful
wine to Him
wine for Him
wine.

Just what came over me I do not know. I cast aside the goblet of wine I had been sipping, got a new one and elbowed my way to the jars. I dipped the goblet in and put the now fragrant liquid to my lips.

And so I sit here writing this outside the city walls in his camp with others who have followed him, this Jesus

man. I am a servant still, that has not changed; for now
I serve Him and the one he serves. But who I am is
different for having taste this new wine, for having
heard his new words, for having felt and followed,
risking everything, his new life.

With him I am no longer
Agathon the eunuch Agathon
the sterile Agathon
the useless unloved unblessed
Agathon the water.
With him I am now
Agathon the bold
creative giving
Agathon the rich and useful
loved and loving risking Agathon
renamed with Jesus
Agathon the wine.

Where I go from here is uncertain. I quite likely will
return to my city of Cana and to my job there. But no
matter where I go or what I do I know who it is that I
follow and it is different - I am different.

I, Agathon the renamed, write this with my own
hand. May you who find and read this scroll break
bread and drink that same wine together, that danger-
ous, caring and confronting Jesus-wine, that wine that
changes minds and lives, that wine that changes names.

Luke 4.1-13

And Jesus, full of the Holy Spirit, returned from the Jordan, and was led by the Spirit for forty days in the wilderness, tempted by the devil. And he ate nothing in those days; and when they were ended, he was hungry.

The devil said to him, "If you are the Son of God, command this stone to become bread." And Jesus answered him, "It is written, 'Man shall not live by bread alone.'"

And the devil took him up and showed him all the kingdoms of the world in a moment of time, and said to him, "To you I will give all this authority and their glory; for it has been delivered to me, and I give it to whom I will. If you, then, will worship me, it shall all be yours." And Jesus answered him, "It is written,'You shall worship the Lord your God, and him only shall you serve.'"

And he took him to Jerusalem, and set him on the pinnacle of the temple, and said to him, "If you are the Son of God, throw yourself down from here; for it is written, 'He will give his angels charge of you, to guard you,'and 'On their hands they will bear you up, lest you strike your foot against a stone.'"

And Jesus answered him, "It is said, 'You shall not tempt the Lord your God.'" And when the devil had ended every temptation, he departed from him until an opportune time.

SYDNEY AND MORTIMER
IN HELL

It was hotter than Austin in hell one day as two devils sat plotting and arguing. Mortimer, the older and taller of the two, pounded his calloused fist on the thick stone table and yelled at his smaller, younger companion:

"I don't believe this Sydney! How could he have chosen YOU for this job?"

"Hey...How could he NOT have chosen me, Mort, ol' boy? Ya know what I mean? I mean, after all, who's got the record for most consecutive hits on a sinner, souls batted in and religious bases stolen?"

"Records! What do records tell you?! Nothing! What this job takes is finesse. And I, I who have been practicing, rehearsing, dreaming of this moment for years, decades, centuries, I am positively mortified..."

"Appropriate choice of words..."

"Don't interrupt me, brimstone breath. Where was I. Oh yes. I am mortified that YOU have been chosen out of all the capable talent around here to be the one to tempt...uh.. You Know Who..."

"Whatsamatter, Mort, chicken to say it? You mean JESUS!!!"

"BE QUIET you dimwitted forktail! Every time you say that name three or four more souls down here get away from us. And you KNOW how Lucifer gets when he loses a few."

"That's okay. When he sees what I've got planned for JESUS..."

"There go some more..."

"Let them go! When he sees what I've got planned - and, more importantly, sees the results - he'll let thousands go to back me up. I'm going after the Big One."

"Oh, my dear Sydney, I can see you haven't given this much thought. Just what is it that you have in mind to do?"

"Well...I wouldn't share this with just anybody, Mort, but you and me go way back."

"Yes, we have been through Hell together."

"So I can tell you this in the strictest confidence."

"Be assured you can trust me, Sydney."

"I plan to give him the triple play. I'm going to hit him with the three most basic and biggest temptations of all..."

"Madonna, Miata, and Moet Champagne?"

"That's your problem, Mortimer, you don't think *big* enough. I'm going to tempt him with the most reliable trio in history - sensuality, power and prerogative."

"I must admit that's very good, even for you, Sydney; but do you realize just when it is that you're assigned to go after him?"

"Of course, Mort. It's right after he gets baptized."

"But don't you think that's right at the height of his resistance?"

"That's why Lucifer chose ME for this job, Morty. You sound like a typical Christian."

"Don't you insult *me*, fireface."

"Well, it's true. You sound just like those folks who think that they're most holy and religious and pious right after prayer or sacraments or something - when in fact that's just when they're most vulnerable to us. Lucifer knows that's the best time for us to strike. That's why he set up the appointment for me right after JESUS..."

"There go some more souls, you little..."

"...right after he's baptized and comes out of the wilderness."

"Well, supposing you're right, supposing it is the most vulnerable time for him; still, how are you going to tempt him with sensuality? I don't think he'd fall for the usual 'Buy a lady a drink' number."

"Of course he wouldn't, Mort. That's why I'm gonna be real sub-tile with him."

"I am afraid to ask."

"Ya see, I know he's gonna be real hungry having been out in the desert all that time. I know that he's gonna have one thing on his mind from going through all that without enchiladas, without barbecue, without Lone Star beer. It's just like normal people, Mort. Everybody's hungry for something. Lots of folks have been hungry for something a long, long time."

"I see. So all we have to do is present that thing to them in an attractive way and, since they're guided by their hunger, they'll snap it up and we've got them!"

"Right Mort!"

"It won't work, Sydney."

"What?"

"It won't work, Sydney. You tell this guy to change some pebbles into pumpernickel and he'll choke you with a loaf of Texas French Bread. He won't buy it, buddy."

"You underestimate my persuasive powers, Mortimer, and you overestimate his resistance. Remember his humanity - he's just like the rest of them and it works like a charm on the rest of them. Feed that hunger - and they're ours."

"I hope you're right - but I doubt it. So what's in store for the second part of your triple play?"

"Ah, they get more beautiful as they progress, Mort. The second one is an even more wonderful temptation. The second one is *power*."

"What're you going to do, offer him a job as football coach for Texas A&M?"

"Bigger than that, furnacemouth."

"Turn him into Gary Trudeau?"

"No."

"Mike Wallace?"

"No."

"Not Oprah Winfrey?"

"No no no no no. None of the above. I'll simply tell him that if he'll worship me I'll make him king of the world. Everybody wants to be king of the world, Mort. Promise them popularity, fame, wealth, tell them they'll be well liked, not even necessarily loved - just well liked and looked up to and they'll follow you anywhere!"

"But that's because everybody, present company excepted of course, thinks that deep down underneath all the exterior facade, they are basically unacceptable, unlovable, unwanted. They think that if people really got to know them they wouldn't be liked."

"And you think Jesus..?"

"Lost a few more Syd."

"Put 'em on my tab. As I was saying, you think *he's* any different? You think *he's* not feeling alone and misunderstood and hunted and a misfit and hurting for acceptance? You forget this guy's been misinterpreted and stalked since the day after he was born. He's no different than the rest of them, Mortimer. All I have to do is offer him unlimited acceptance and authority. He'll jump at it - they always do."

"Oh brother, are you in trouble. Can I ask a defeatist question, Sydney old fiend?"

"Go right ahead, Mort. Jealousy will get you nowhere."

"What happens if you blow this assignment?"

"That's unthinkable."

"So was the Titanic. But this is pure conjecture of course."

"Of course. Well...on the outside, impossible, highly improbably, unlikely and obscene chance that this strategy...uh...doesn't work out; in that case I am banished to the absolute lowest pit of hell."

"You mean....you mean that you would have to spend eternity arguing with all those lawyer politicians?"

"Worse. I'd spend the rest of my existence trying to convince all the clergy down there that God didn't route them through Houston."

"Oh dear, Sydney. I hope the third part of your strategy is better than the other two."

"It's the best yet, Mort. This last one appeals to the basest most fundamental, ingrained and morally predictable weakness of humanity."

"What's that, Sydney, the need for oat bran?"

"Of course not, demonbrain! It is the weakness of *prerogative.*"

"'Prerogative?'"

"Certainly, Mortimer. Human beings, poor lost souls that they are, doom themselves with their constant search for specialness, for individuality, for the feeling that the rules don't apply to them because they are different. They expect miracles, demand healings and assume *their* prayers carry more weight."

"I hate to admit it, Sydney, but you've hit on a winner there. People like to think they are the chosen people, or that because they are followers of.... of...."

"*SAY* it Mort...of JESUS!"

"There go some more souls on your conscience. Yes, because they follow him, or claim to, they expect that the normal rules of disease, accident, misfortune or even death should somehow not apply to them."

"Yes, yes! Isn't it wonderful?!?! And their demand for prerogative, or even better, the assumption they have it, is played out in pious behavior to command deference from those less fortunate souls than themselves."

"But how are you going to tempt him with that one, Sydney? It's so obvious!"

"Same way we do with everyone else, Mort. Appeal to his vanity, appeal to his ego, make it look like he doesn't trust God if he doesn't take the dare. I'm going to...well, here, I'd better whisper it to you. You never can tell who's listening."

(whisper, whisper)

"THE PINNACLE OF THE TEMPLE!!!"

"SSSSSSSSHHHHHHHHHHHHHH!!! Keep it under your horns, Mort!"

"Sydney, if you take him up there do you know what he'll probably say to you?"

"Of course I do, he'll say...."

"He'll say 'If you don't get us down from here I'm gonna throw up.' Or words to that effect. *It's not gonna work, Sydney!*"

"O ye of little faith, Mortimer. I have tried these out on hundreds of thousands before this one. They all are foolproof temptations, and when coupled with my own obviously superior talents I will personally deliver to our fearless leader Lucifer the soul of, as you so aptly put it, 'You Know Who.'"

"Oh go ahead and say it, Sydney. A few souls more or less at this point will hardly besmirch your supposedly impressive record."

"Okay. I will personally deliver to Lucifer the eternally enslaved soul of JESUS!"

(Mortimer vanishes.)

"Mortimer??? Mortimer!! Where did that old devil go to? How rude! Guess he just couldn't take it anymore, listening to such a well thought out plan. No wonder *I* was chosen over him." (Looks at his watch) "Holy Clergypit! It's time for Jesus to come out of the wilderness and I haven't even pressed my tail yet. I'm so excited, I can hardly wait. Just imagine me sitting up there for eternity right beside Lucifer, deciding where in Hell to send everybody." (Thinks a second.) "Of course, if it doesn't work....all those clergy... What's the matter with me? I'm starting to sound like Mortimer." (Looks around.) "Poor old Mortimer. I wonder, where *did* he go?"

Mark 6.45-52

Immediately after the feeding of the five thousand, Jesus made his disciples get into the boat and go before him to the other side, to Bethsaida, while he dismissed the crowd. And after he had taken leave of them, he went up on the mountain to pray.

And when evening came, the boat was out on the sea, and he was alone on the land. And he saw that they were making headway painfully, for the wind was against them. And about the fourth watch of the night he came to them, walking on the sea. He meant to pass by them, but when they saw him walking on the sea they thought it was a ghost, and cried out: for they all saw him, and were terrified.

But immediately he spoke to them and said, "Take heart, it is I; have no fear." And he got into the boat with them and the wind ceased. and they were utterly astounded, for they did not understand about the loaves, but their hearts were hardened.

Letter from Miriam

I have to write this down. I have no choice. I am so overwhelmed with feeling that I need to get it out of me, to express it, to set it forth so that others can read it and know what happened out here in this otherwise forsaken land.

I suppose I should say that my name is Miriam. I am the daughter of a shepherd here in this small town. But I am luckier than most. I learned this bit of writing from working in the town taking care of the ruler's children. I know I am not supposed to know these things, that reading and writing are reserved for the rich and the powerful and primarily for men. But I have always been possessed by the demon of curiosity - and it was that demon that brought me out there that day.

I first heard of this Jesus when the crowds started gathering over on the hill outside of town. I took the ruler's children with me as I always do when some new magician or prophet comes around. It is good for them to see how those foolish people behave. So my curiosity led me there late in the afternoon.

I arrived just as his disciples were begging him to do something to feed all the multitudes who had been there listening to him. And that's when my curiosity really got hooked. All the other people of his kind would have welcomed the opportunity to show off their tricks and use the occasion to build up their own popularity and power. But Jesus told the disciples to go feed them themselves. It was as though he told them they had the power to do it and didn't need him to rescue them.

Then, after he blessed the bread and broke it, we all were fed - with some left over to take home to others. Then he did another thing that was amazing to me. Instead of telling everyone what a great person he was and asking them all to follow him and worship him - he sent us all away! First he sent his disciples away in the boat, and then he dismissed us all as if to say: "Now you go and do that same thing with each other."

Well, I certainly couldn't leave after that. I hung back by myself and sent the children home with another woman from the town. I wanted to talk to this Jesus, to touch him and hear his voice and have him touch me too. I know it was a brazen thing to do, to approach a man like that, but I was so moved, so attracted to this difference that I had to know more. How could I know that my demon curiosity would show me more than I could imagine?

I watched as his disciples put out on the lake. I was a bit worried for them as I looked at the approaching storm clouds on the horizon. I wondered that Jesus didn't worry too. But he seemed always to assume they could handle anything that came upon them just as well has he could. In fact, he seemed to have more faith in them than they had in him - *or* in themselves. I was surprised that he didn't go with them. Then I was glad when I saw him go up on the mountain by himself.

I started to approach him but hesitated because he seemed lost in thought. He mumbled some things and seemed to be talking to himself, flailing his arms about and accentuating his loud words with movements. He looked like he was arguing with somebody, or at times pleading with somebody, and finally, almost in desperation it seemed, he sat down on a large rock, crossed his knees and cupped his chin in his hands and stared into the approaching darkness gradually overtaking the lake.

By now I was getting a little scared. But I am always amazed how much scare and excitement are so intertwined. The more I watched him the more I wanted to walk right out there and talk with him, listen to him, ask him millions of questions. Just as I overcame my fear somewhat, he stood and walked back down the mountain toward the shore, constantly looking out at the boat which was becoming less and less visible in the shadows.

I followed him down the path and, thinking this would be my last chance to talk to him alone, I bravely

- well, sort of bravely - well, actually my knees were a little shaky on the sand - but nonetheless I slowly, cautiously approached this powerful man who seemed not to want the power others saw in him.

Before I could speak he spoke to me. Without looking at me, still staring out at the now churning lake he held up his hand to me.

"Shhhhh," he said. "Can you hear them?"

"Just barely," I whispered. "They seem to be shouting, but the wind is getting so strong it almost drowns..."

"Bad choice of words," he said.

"Sorry," I said. "I mean the wind covers up..."

"I know what you mean."

He turned for a moment and looked at me. I must say I nearly fainted. His eyes were so soft and yet so, I don't know, so understanding. He reached out his hand for me to take it and he looked back out at the water. I touched his hand and found it warm even with the cold wind blowing with more and more fierceness off the lake. As we held hands there, staring out at the storm I felt like a little child holding onto my Daddy's hand. But I also felt like a mother holding the hand of one of the children in the town who wanted reassurance and nurturing. And - and this is incredible - I felt as though I was holding the hand of a friend, an equal. Though I knew he must be much more powerful than I, it seemed as if he conveyed that we were equally strong.

Standing there beside him, I was amazed to feel that I was giving as much to him as he gave to me. I never before thought that a prophet *needed anything* from others, or would accept anything especially from a member of society who was considered chattel. I guess I felt something I'd never felt before - accepted for myself and able to accept him for himself.

We stood that way for what seemed half of forever before he spoke.

"Thanks for following me down here."

"You knew I was there all along?"

"Yes, of course." He smiled. "You're not exactly the Spy Queen you know. Sound travels easily out here."

"Then why didn't you say something before this?"

"I was busy. I had some thinking to do before coming down here."

I was shocked. Here I was talking to this perfect stranger like I'd known him for years. He seemed to be so vulnerable and willing to tell me his deepest thoughts. It was so overwhelming that I wanted to run away. I would imagine he has that effect on everybody. Anyway, he must have sensed my feeling.

"Please don't go yet," he said. "Very seldom do people stay around to talk after such a gathering as that. And even less often does someone risk getting this close to me."

"It is scary," I ventured.

"It needn't be. It's like those men out there in the boat."

"I can hardly see them now for the rain and wind," I said. "This storm is frightening to me too."

67

"That's the real trouble, isn't it?" he said, staring at the churning water. "People can't see through the storm because of their own fear. People won't reach out to touch the warmth and love of each other because of fear. People won't come to know God because of fear."

He smiled and said: "If only they would learn they're fearing the wrong things."

"What do you mean?"

"I'm afraid too," he said. I'm afraid of boredom and complacency. I'm afraid of power misused and freedom become license. I'm afraid of prejudice and hatred and lies and war.

"And others? What do you think they fear?"

"They fear themselves. They fear they are not good or wise enough, strong or powerful enough, popular or rich enough. And because of the fear they don't see through the storms of their lives, they don't use the power, the love, the wisdom they have to still the waters and use the wind to their advantage."

"And you...what will you do about all that?"

"The only thing I can do. Show them the way. Show them what they're capable of. Tell them about themselves. Give warmth and strength just as you are giving to me now."

He shook his head.

"See how painfully they move in the storm? See how they yell and argue and blame each other? Just as groups, cities, states, countries do. Maybe if I go to them..."

I looked around the shore, then back out to the water.

He smiled and looked at me.

"I know there's no boat here," he said.

Not knowing what to say I smiled back at him. He laughed and said: "Don't pay very close attention to what you're going to see here. It can be interpreted a lot of ways."

"What are you talking about?"

"I'm going out there on the lake to be with my friends in their need."

My eyes widened.

"Some people will record that I walked on the water," he said. That's one possibility."

"What are others?"

"You tell me."

"Maybe it just looked that way to them. Maybe you're a ghost. Maybe you're a good swimmer. Maybe you got a ride on a dolphin's back. Maybe you flew. Maybe..."

Jesus winked at me. "Maybe I just knew where the rocks were," he laughed.

"But doesn't it make a big difference which one it was?"

"No, not at all! That's where people get misled, trying to figure out what exactly happened. What matters isn't *how* it happened - what matters is *that* it happened. What matters is that my Father goes to people exactly when 'they're making headway painfully' in the midst of their storms."

The wind grew stronger and we began to get drenched by the pouring rain.

"I need to go now," he said. "Thank you for being here with me, for holding me and taking my hand. I need nurturing too, though people don't want to see me that way. I'm glad you did. Thanks."

I barely managed to get "You're welcome" out of my mouth before he leaned over, kissed me, and let go of my hand. Then he turned and walked into the midst of the raging waters.

I can only tell you what I saw. Others may write this down in different ways. I can only put into words the vision that appeared before me. Just as he said, he managed to get out to their boat. Actually, it looked as though he didn't even mean to stop there but was going to the other side to meet them. I don't know how he did it. All I know is it didn't matter to me. I felt such calm inside though the storm was raging around me that I *did* see through the storm and hear the voices of the men in the boat. And I was amazed.

At first they thought it was a ghost. They did not expect this man to come to them, even though they knew him better than anyone else; even though they had traveled and talked and lived and broken bread and drunk wine with him for many months before.

He spoke to them and said "Take heart, it is I. You need have no fear." It was as if to say, "Trust me. I'm here with you. Together we'll make it through this storm too." And as soon as he got into the boat with them, the wind died down, though the rain kept pounding in torrents.

I stood there a while watching, wondering. Even through the rain I could see the look on some of their faces. They didn't know what to think. It even looked like some of them resented him for being there, for again telling them they had it in them to calm their storms, to steady their boats, if they would only accept him and fear the things that he feared.

Then, in a moment, they were out of sight. As though in a daze I stood, still feeling his warmth in the now drizzling rain, hearing his laughter, knowing I could never be the same again.

I was shaken from my thoughts by a familiar voice shouting my name from the hilltop where Jesus had been earlier. I turned to see my father sliding down the muddy hill to meet me. I knew he was worried and wondered what in the world I was doing there, soaked to the skin, with a strange look on my face. As he came to me I reached out my arms to him and hugged him - and I cried.

Weeks have passed now since I saw Jesus in the storm. Sometimes I can't tell if it was a dream or was real. Then something happens in my life that I think I can't handle and I remember the boat and the words and his actions there.

And so I write this letter, I know not to whom, hoping some day someone might find it and know him, or the God he represented, as I did that strange afternoon, as I have since then, as I do now. Take his hand not only to *be* strengthened, but to strengthen, not only to *be* nurtured, but to nurture, not only to *be* loved, but to love. But beware of him. He will demand of you what he demanded of me and of his disciples in that boat. He will demand that we calm our own storms, that we use our own gifts, that we laugh at our own assumptions about him and about ourselves, that we fear what *he* fears.

I, Miriam, write this with my own hand. May those who read and hear this story tell it again and again and again.

ZECHARIAH 9.9-12

Rejoice greatly, O daughter of Zion!
  Shout aloud, O daughter of Jerusalem!
Lo, your king comes to you;
  triumphant and victorious is he,
humble and riding on an ass,
  on a colt the foal of an ass.
I will cut off the chariot from Ephraim
  and the war horse from Jerusalem;
and the battle bow shall be cut off,
  and he shall command peace to the nations;
his dominion shall be from sea to sea,
  and from the River to the ends of the earth.
As for you also, because of the blood of my covenant
    with you,
  I will set your captives free from the waterless pit.
Return to your stronghold, O prisoners of hope;
  today I declare that I will restore to you double.

Prisoners of Hope

I am Zechariah, son of Iddo. I came from a priestly family that survived the exile. My career spanned a short two years and so I am sure that most people are not familiar at all with my book in what is today called the Old Testament. I received all my divine revelation through angels rather than directly from God. I was also the first one to use the term "The Satan" to describe an adversary of God. Suffice it to say *that* phrase has gotten blown all out of proportion.

I am writing this because this section of Scripture - this chapter nine - contains words that have interested me for centuries, and I want to make certain that they are understood, though *I* did not write chapter nine. I only wrote up to eight. Nine to fourteen were written by somebody else using my name. But it is close enough to what I said previously for me to explain it. I do not expect that what I am about to say will be palatable to everyone reading this, but that goes with the prophetic territory. It has always been interesting to me that people think it is possible to witness to God's word and stay out of trouble with the world, when in fact the two are almost always mutually exclusive.

Chapter nine heralds the coming of the messiah. And look how he is coming - quite different from the kinds of power the world worships and respects. He's arriving "triumphant," "victorious," AND "humble", while most of our leaders and power dealers come triumphant, smiling and arrogant. They think, like most people actually, that their power is entirely their own making. The messiah knows better. His power is from God, and he is thus able to be triumphant *and* humble. I wonder what would happen if this nation celebrated its victories with humility instead of self-serving parades? But to do that we would have to know what victory really was in the first place, wouldn't it?

So the messiah comes upon us triumphant "and" humble. He also comes with a universalism that transcends petty denominationalism and anachronistic nationalism. He reunites the world, north and south Israel, along with the world from sea to sea.

That means that in *God's* kingdom we may be sitting down at table with a Zen Buddhist, a Russian nationalist, a Middle Eastern revolutionary or even a card carrying member of the Moral Majority. God through the messiah is unifying beyond the phony boundaries we arbitrarily set to reassure ourselves that we are right and true and good, beyond the limits of our myopic judgmentalness, beyond our self-serving images of who is chosen and who is not. The messiah's arms are outstretched to all the world as he bids them come to the banquet.

And his first word to us is to *command peace*. I have always thought that an interesting way of putting it - "he shall *command peace*". To tell you the truth, even though the writer of this passage used my name, I am not sure what he meant by that. He might have meant that the messiah's presence itself commanded peace. Or he might have envisioned the messiah saying "STOP" to international policies based on Mutually Assured Destruction (MAD); saying "STOP" to ethnocentric arrogance growing out of accidents of skin color, language or religious belief.

In any case, peace is *commanded* - not requested. The messiah does not send out personalized, embossed invitations to which we may or may not RSVP. Rather, we are *commanded* to be at peace because that is the way God's kingdom is meant to be.

Next, the prophet who writes in my name says that, because of God's covenant, because of God's promise of restoration and renewal, God will set the captives free. And then he uses a phrase I wish I *could* take credit for. He calls us "prisoners of hope." What a wonderfully descriptive term! I can just envision persons held captive by their *hopefulness* living in eager expectation, refusing to bow to the seductive idols of despair and aggrandizement, ignoring the faddish demands of societal peers to conform, condone and consume — and all of this because of *certain hopefulness* about their covenant relationship with God.

But are we really prisoners of hope? When we are honest, just exactly what is *our* specific, personal prison? Are we prisoners of depression, prisoners of success or power, prisoners of popularity, prisoners of sensuality, prisoners of piety or suffering, prisoners of sentimental religiosity or intellectualism, or prisoners of vengeance and bitterness? I, Zechariah, son of Iddo the priest, have been around a long time, and I have seen very few true prisoners of hope.

There is one other thing I want to write before I close this epistle, and that has to do with being a prophet. Most people think prophets spend all their time forecasting the future. People want to believe that, because they think if we are talking about some far off event there is plenty of time to put off doing anything about it. But that is another lie.

What I talked about in my first eight chapters and what the other people following talked about is not *future* oriented at all. Rather, it is centered in the *here and now* - in the *present*. That means when we are called to emulate the messiah by being triumphant, victorious AND humble, we are to be that NOW.

Imagine what it would mean for us to be triumphant, victorious and humble in all areas of social, political, economic and religious life. And it is clear to me at least that that is exactly what we are called to do now that the messiah has come — unless of course we do not believe that his kingdom has begun.

Likewise, we are to live as a united world, under a universalism that transcends national and denominational boundaries. If all we see is the borderlines between continents, between ideologies, between East, Northwest, South and Northeast Austin, then we are living as though the messiah has not yet come into the world. We are called to live as one world NOW - not as an idealistic dream of what might be, but rather as a reflection of the reality of what has taken place with Jesus' coming.

Also, as unpopular as it is, we are called to *command* peace *now.* Not to ask for it, not to wish for it, not to stand idly by and pray that God will make it happen magically. No, we are called to *command* it - to command it of our legislators, to command it of our civic and religious and military leaders, to command it of ourselves. This may be the most important task of all. Given our penchant for power and destruction, it may in fact be the first priority.

Finally, the daily task, even the hourly task to which we are called is perhaps the simplest and most difficult. We are called to live as prisoners of hope NOW. We are called to use hope as our boundary, to have hope as the only thing which limits us, to bind our actions with the one thing that goes counter to every other message our society expects from us — hope.

Many people will confuse optimism with hope. But the words are not the same. Indeed, optimism is a dungeon deep with despair and desolation. To be hopeful is to be realistically faithful to the promise of restoration God has made to us and to behave as though it has already occurred.

Well, enough of my words. I had meant this to be only a short letter. May all who read this experience triumphs and victories as reason for humility this very day. May God guide us all to a vision of a world beyond arbitrary barriers so that we will use our considerable personal resources to order our individual, social, corporate and national lives to witness to God's universally outstretched arms.

May we live this day and each day as it comes in such a way as to command peace in all our doings, firmly, consistently, assertively; knowing that peace is not the absence of conflict but the presence of God.

Finally, focusing on the promise of the messiah, may we abandon and so escape our current prisons of power, popularity, security, piety, nationalism, bitterness or optimism, and become instead prisoners of unbounded freedom, prisoners of unconditional love, prisoners of the eternal present. Indeed, may we with all our courage become true prisoners of hope.

Signed,

Zechariah ben Iddo, Prophet of YHWH

Exodus 16.2-4, 9-15

And the whole congregation of the people of Israel murmured against Moses and Aaron in the wilderness, and said to them, "Would that we had died by the hand of the Lord in the land of Egypt, when we sat by the fleshpots and ate bread to the full; for you have brought us out into this wilderness to kill this whole assembly with hunger."

The Lord said to Moses, "Behold, I will rain bread from heaven for you; and the people shall go out and gather a day's portion every day, that I may prove them, whether they will walk in my law or not.

And Moses said to Aaron, "Say to the whole congregation of the people of Israel, 'Come near before the Lord, for he has heard your murmurings.'" And as Aaron spoke to the whole congregation of the people of Israel, they looked toward the wilderness, and behold, the glory of the Lord appeared in the cloud. And the Lord said to Moses, "I have heard the murmurings of the people of Israel; say to them, 'At twilight you shall eat flesh, and in the morning you shall be filled with bread; then you shall know that I am the Lord your God.'"

In the evening quails came up and covered the camp; and in the morning dew lay round about the camp. And when the dew had gone up, there was on the face of the wilderness a fine, flake-like thing, fine as hoarfrost on the ground. When the people of Israel saw it, they said to one another, "What is it?" For they did not know what it was. And Moses said to them, "It is the bread which the Lord has given you to eat.

HEART MURMURS

We sit in darkness   Yes
as we have sat in darkness many years   I know you have.
waiting for you to save us.   Yes.
Where are you when we need you,   Here.
want you,   Here.
demand your presence in our lives?   I am here with you.
We sat in slavery to politics,   Chains.
traditional religion, social status   Chains.
and an economy aimed at war   All of those chains
                                                        bind you.

and waited for you to save us.   Yes.
Our people died as slaves   Died.
to those obscene gods we worshiped;   Why did you
                                                    worship *them*
gods that shaped us, held us,   Stripped you naked.
stripped us of our dignity,   Deceived you.
cheated us and made us bow down   Bow too low.
to popularity, power, lust, and   Worst of all.

complacent boredom with ourselves.   You lost yourselves
                                                        then.

We were lost, God, and so we followed   Follow.

the messenger you sent to lead us out   Follow.

of this wasteland into the place of   Follow still.

peace and work and fairness.   And I did.

And we did.   I know.

So here we sit again   Again?

wondering where you are   I'm here.

now that we are again hungry   I am here.

and dying in this, another wasteland.   Here.

We yell at you   I know.

and want a sign that you are with us   Yes.

and that you hear us   I hear.

and that you care   I care.

and that we will not die   You will not die.

in this god-forsaken place.   You will not die
                                                        there.

We trusted you   I trusted you.

and left the comfort of that slavery   Comfort.

and the certitude of that enemy   Certitude.

for the risk of life with you.   It is a risk.

And now we want you   I want you.

to come to us with answers in our need.   Your need. My need.

Tell us what to do, God,   What to do?

about abortion and death of those we

                                                love;   Love.

war and famine and hostages;   Give.

racial hatred and national prejudice.   Trust.

Show us the way out of this wilderness   Follow.
and into that promised land   Follow.
you promised us so long ago.   Yesterday is now.
Be God, God,   I am.
if you are really there.   I am.

What is this?   It is bread.
What are you doing   Feeding you.
surrounding us with abundance   I am with you.
of food and friends and wonder?   I am with you,
                                                                as I said.

What has this abundance to do   Everything.
with our problems?   You asked me for it.
You still don't understand, God   Oh.
what we need.   You are in need.
We ask you for help   Help I give.
and you give us sustenance.   Yes.
We ask you for direction   You direct
                                                     yourselves.

and you give us bread to eat.   Nurturing.
What kind of God are you   Yours.
anyway?   Your God.
We did not look for this   Bread.
answer from you.   Take my bread.
We did not know what it was   Look now.
because we did not expect it.   Bread.
Surrounded with your abundance   Your abundance.
we ignored your answer   My love.

to our murmuring

Talking to me.

in this wilderness

The desert of your soul.

till your prophet told us what it was.

His eyes are better.

We will take the sustenance

Thank you.

for now.

Now is all there is.

We will take the manna, the bread,

Thank you.

for now.

Now is all we have.

But we wonder why

And I also wonder why

you do not understand

you have not yet
                caught on.

that we want

I give you all you need.

more from you?

I give you all I am.

Do you not hear us,

I hear. Do you not
                listen?

listen to our crying out for you?

I cry with you, for you,
                for me.

We eat this bread now

Take it.

feed it to each other

Break it.

fill our hungry bodies

Be it.

with your hoarfrost manna.

Word.

We have eaten, Lord

Be filled.

and we are full of your spiritbread.

Be filled with me.

This barren desert is a jungle now

Full.

lush and green and giving

Receiving and giving

to us meeting all our needs.

Your needs and wants.

Forgive us, Lord

I forgive you.

for our hasty judgments	Judge all.
our blind demands	See now.
our incessant asking.	Ask again.
But you know us well enough to know	I know.
that we will ask again	When?
when the bread wears off	Is used.
and we think we are once more	Alone.
alone in the wilderness	There is no wilderness in me.
inside our lives and souls and land.	Be within me.
So send your prophet still	I send them.
to open eyes and remind us	I recall with you.
who we are, who you are	Who I am together.
with us, for us, in us.	We together.
Keep the bread coming, Lord.	I bake daily.
Feed us, fill our hunger	I will offer.
till we murmur	You will murmur.
once again.	I understand.
Amen.	And also with you.

Acts 9.1-19a

But Saul, still breathing threats and murder against the disciples of the Lord, went to the high priest and asked him for letters to the synagogues at Damascus, so that if he found any belonging to the Way, men or women, he might bring them bound to Jerusalem. Now as he journeyed he approached Damascus, and suddenly a light from heaven flashed about him.

And he fell to the ground and heard a voice saying to him, "Saul, Saul, why do you persecute me?" And he said, "Who are you, Lord?" And he said, "I am Jesus, whom you are persecuting; but rise and enter the city, and you will be told what you are to do."

The men who were traveling with him stood speechless, hearing the voice but seeing no one. Saul arose from the ground; and when his eyes were opened, he could see nothing; so they led him by the hand and brought him into Damascus. And for three days he was without sight, and neither ate nor drank.

Now there was a disciple at Damascus named Ananias. The Lord said to him in a vision, "Ananias." And he said, "Here I am, Lord." And the Lord said to him, "Rise and go to the street called Straight, and inquire in the house of Judas for a man of Tarsus named Saul; for behold, he is praying, and he has seen a man named Ananias come in and lay his hands on him so that he might regain his sight."

But Ananias answered, "Lord, I have heard from many about this man, how much evil he has done to thy saints at Jerusalem; and here he has authority from the chief priests to bind all who call upon thy name." But the Lord said to him, "Go, for he is a chosen instrument of mine to carry my name before the Gentiles and kings and the sons of Israel; for I will show him how much he must suffer for the sake of my name."

So Ananias departed and entered the house. And laying his hands on him he said, "Brother Saul, the Lord Jesus, who appeared to you on the road by which you came, has sent me that you may regain your sight and be filled with the Holy Spirit." And immediately something like scales fell from his eyes and he regained his sight. Then he rose and was baptized, and took food and was strengthened.

For several days he was with the disciples at Damascus.

Three Days in Saul's Head

"Saul arose from the ground; and when his eyes were opened he could see nothing...and for three days he was without sight and neither ate nor drank."

Day One

I AM FURIOUS!! WHAT AM I DOING HERE?! WHAT HAS HAPPENED TO MY EYES?! WHAT HAS HAPPENED TO MY THROAT?! NO WORDS WILL COME OUT AND NO FOOD CAN GO DOWN!! I STUMBLE AROUND THIS TINY ROOM, BANGING MY SHINS ON GOD KNOWS WHAT ALL; BED, TABLE, CHAIR, RUNNING INTO WALLS I CAN'T SEE AND PEOPLE I DON'T KNOW. THIS IS UNFAIR!! I AM STRUCK DOWN FOR NO REASON!! IT IS HATEFUL, MEAN AND DISHONEST!! I WILL PERSECUTE THEM ALL THE MORE FOR BRINGING THIS ON ME. I KNEW THOSE CHRISTIANS WERE DANGEROUS. THIS CONFIRMS IT!! THEY ARE SORCERERS, EVIL MAGICIANS, AND I WILL GET THEM BACK FOR THIS. WAIT AND SEE!!

SEE?! SEE?! My God, what if I can no longer see? What if I am now blind for life? What if their spell, their Christian evil spell is forever? What will I do then? Who will follow me then? How can a blind man give orders? I will have to beg...ME...SAUL...A BLIND BEGGAR!!! I AM FURIOUS!!! I CANNOT BELIEVE THIS IS HAPPENING TO ME!!! No.! Stop. Wait a minute, Saul. Calm down. Sit down. Where is the chair? I know..I know it's here somewhere ... OUCH .... DAMN...here... here it is. Maybe if I sit down, be calm, maybe I can figure something....come up with some...

What happened? That's it!...Go over what happened. How did I get here? I was on my way to Damascus. We were talking of how we would search out any belonging to the Way...search them out...bind them in chains and bring them back to Jerusalem for trial. We had just come within sight of the city when...what was it?...A blinding flash of light. It was as though the sun exploded in my face. I fell to my knees, clutching my eyes, covering their burning pain with my hands, asking who this was who had overcome me. Then there was that voice, that haunting voice. He said it was him whom I persecute. But how can that be? He is dead. Those stories are only rumours, they incite to riot, they are the stuff of which revolution is made. They must be suppressed. It is a hoax. But then...but then there was that voice...that strange commanding voice.

My men brought me here, led me here by the hand like a helpless infant. They brought me to this house and here I am a prisoner of this infernal darkness. I see nothing, taste nothing, do nothing. I HATE THIS BLINDNESS. It immobilizes me. I am a busy man. I have work to do, places to go, people to meet. I am important. I have a hectic schedule. In this darkness I am stopped. I am nothing. I am nobody.

I do not understand this. It makes no sense. I am a religious man; a devout man. I say the prayers. I keep the rituals. I study Torah. This...this... blindness ...this insanity...this ridicule happens to other people but not to me; not to Saul. NO! Not to ME! I am Saul the faithful, Saul the devout, Saul the committed. MASTER OF THE UNIVERSE, WHY DO YOU MAKE ME ALSO SAUL THE BLIND?!

I am suddenly so tired. My whole body aches. I ache with anger. I ache with protest. I ache with hunger. Maybe...maybe if I lie down a while. Where is the bed...ahh...yes...this is it. Perhaps if I just stretch out here a while and think...and think...I wonder. What if that voice... No. He is dead. It is impossible. I am so tired. I am so thirsty. I am...so frightened of this darkness. I am so...alone. If only I could sleep. If only.....sleep. If........sleep.

Day Two

Today is very strange, quite strange....too strange. I feel...how do I feel? A part of me still protests at the blindness. A part of me now welcomes it as calming, silencing my body and my mind from all the chaos that comes with seeing and eating. I am not immobilized. I am stilled. I am stopped. I am quieted.

I awoke this morning hearing rain outside the window; heard it hitting on the roof tiles, listened long as I have never listened to rain before. I stumbled, then walked steadily and with purpose to the window, cupped my hands and splashed the chilling wetness on my face. Drench me, drown me, cleanse me. Master of the Universe, with this water heal my eyes. Give me sight. Return my vision. What have I done that I am struck down like this? I feel remorseful, guilty, saddened because I don't know what to do to atone, not knowing what I have or have not done. The water wakens as it blends in with my tears upon my cheeks.

The thought occurs to me - perhaps there is nothing to do. Perhaps I am to sit and think and wait. When I could see I saw so many things. But now...now that my eyes are stilled I am beginning to see even more. Perhaps my sight got in the way of seeing things clearly...perhaps my sight served merely to confirm what I thought, believed, wanted. My blindness now seems focused on that voice. I cannot get that sound out of my eyes. They focus only on it, repeating, seeing first the flash immobilizing; then some form in it speaking, calling, questioning, commanding.

They bring me food. I cannot eat. I heard them say the owner of this is called Judas. How bizarre! The name of the man who betrayed that Jesus who they called the Christ. That Jesus! How could he be Messiah?? He was not king! He was not powerful! He was crucified and a failure! This is not Messiah! And yet those followers of his...the people of the Way...they say that...no...it cannot be...and yet this voice on the road...how could he talk to me if...

I feel confused. This is too much for me. I am overwhelmed with thought, with feeling, with questions that can never be answered. I am deluged, loose, adrift. There is no place to run. I cannot run from it...from him...from them. This blindness keeps me here. This blindness makes me face him head on. I am a match for him, and he for me. It now is time to struggle. Ask questions I must, ponder more on this I must.

I do not want to sleep. There's too much to consider here, to wrestle with right now. What if...my God...what if in fact...then what...what have I...what am I...what will I...but no...it cannot be...or can it...can it...can it...is it...my God...is it?

My body aches again with tiredness. I will just sit down...lie down here on the bed a while. I must not sleep. I ache with questioning. I ache with disbelief. I ache with struggle, wondering what if it is so? I must

not sleep. I want to stay awake and think. I want to...I
want...I...

Day Three

I am even more frightened today. This day is differ-
ent. Something has happened...is happening. I awoke
this morning feeling the warmth of the sun on my
blanket. My eyelids opened, I know because I felt for
them. Still there is darkness and I am caught between
the silent comfort that darkness brings and the fear that
I will be helpless and dependent forever. I am caught
between this darkness which has befriended me, stilled
me, stopped my assumptions and perceptions and this
same darkness which threatens to encase me, entomb
me always.

They brought me food this morning and although I
cannot eat I was surprised it smelled so good. My
senses told me, maybe later today I might actually feel
like eating. And that is new. Yes...that's it. I have a
sense that things are new - or about to be. I feel like a
small child about to go on a journey, not knowing the
destination but excited about the trip. This is insane.
Nothing has happened. I am still Saul the blind. And
yet...and yet...this is the third day. Those followers of
his say he returned then...on the third day. And if he *is*
Messiah, if he is...

My heart is beating quickly, pounding at the pound-
ing on the door of this house. Who is there? What are
those voices? What are they saying? My God! They are

followers of The Way. They have come for me! Surely they will kill me if they come in here. But my men are there and they are strong. They will...why is there no struggle? Stop them! The door to my room is opening! I have no weapon! I am blind! My God help me!! Save me! No! Don't let them touch me! I am dead! They are leading me out of the room, sitting me down, washing my feet and hands. What is he saying? What is his name? Ananias?

Why does he call me "brother?" Someone - is it this Ananias? - is laying his hands on my head. He says it is Lord Jesus who appeared in that light on the road; it is Lord Jesus who sent him to me to...to regain my sight and be filled with Holy Spirit. His hands on my head are so warm; I am filled with energy, with warmth, with...what is that falling from my eyes? It is like scales dropping, releasing, healing...and...dare I open them? Dare I risk opening them? Do I want to see what lies before me? Do I want to know these men? Do I want to know this Jesus? Part of me wants to hide in blindness, keep it always, stay helpless and angry at its strictures. Darkness, do I want to give you up, forsake your safety, calm entombment, pleasant passive solitude? My answer, three day answer, must be, will be, is....YES.

My eyelids slowly part, wincing against the brightness of the sunlight in the room. I shade them with my hand and squint slowly, cautiously, moving my stiff neck and looking around the room. It is so blurred and out of focus. I cannot see as I did before. There is some impairment and yet...the focus is coming clearer. I see these people all around me. They look as apprehensive as I feel. We are each wondering what the other will do. There is no other choice - I have to smile. They're smiling back. We laugh and break the silence and at last we talk...and wonder.

Once again my whole body aches. I ache with peace. I ache with expectation. I ache with death. I ache with life and spirit. After I am cleansed I will eat some food, slowly. I will learn of him, slowly. Then I will be on my way...on The Way...on his way.

Proverbs 9.1-6

Wisdom has built her house, she has set up her seven pillars.

She has slaughtered her beasts, she has mixed her wine, she has also set her table.

She has sent out her maids to call from the highest places in the town, "Whoever is simple, let him turn in here!"

To him who is without sense she says, "Come, eat of my bread and drink of the wine I have mixed. Leave simpleness and live, and walk in the way of insight."

MS. WIZ

I stopped by Wisdom's house
the other day
To see what might be new with her.
Come in, said she, I see
you read the sign
inviting all the simple to turn in here.
No, I growled, that's not the
reason even though I know I qualify.
And Wisdom smiled a smile that
hugged me and embraced my presence.
Ah, said she, you finally
have come to do more than
observe.
I nodded and she stood
her flowing caftan covering
all the scars upon her body's
aged yet unwrinkled olive skin.
Were you not white and young
when last I came here?
Possibly, said she, my age and
color change as do the eyes of
those who wish to see me.

I understand, said I.
I think you do, said she.

I was told that you have built
your house on seven pillars
is that true?
Almost, she answered, waving
her long arms in gesture,
Actually there are here seven
rooms.
I'd like to see them.
Would you now? she queried.
Would you really, even knowing
that once seeing them
you never could go back?
All within me trembled
as the words formed and fell off
my lips announcing
It is time.
Perhaps it is, said she, so
I will lead you.

Taking my hand in hers
she twirled around
her caftan swirling
like a billowed sail
and said
This is the living room
It is to dance, to sing
to talk and listen in.
In this bright room
the pulse of life beats
by the minute, day and year.
It is a room for feeling
crying, laughing, warming
growing ending and

beginning.
Yes, I said, it is a light and living
room.
I'm glad you like it
Wisdom said
Now come with me and see the next one.

We advanced through curtained
portals to a smaller steamy
place that smelled of perfumed
waters.
Light streamed in through
panes transparent in the ceiling
and reflected in the pool before us.
What is this? I asked
What would you guess? she said
and flushed the object next to her.
A bathroom in the house of Wisdom?
What wise house would be without one?
Here we bathe and rest and swim
our bodies cleansed and pores unburdened
of the toxins that we store each day.
This is a room of sweat and salt
smells mingled with the swirling sweetness
of the waters for refreshing and renewing.
Can we stay here?
Not until the tour is finished.
There are other rooms to show you.
Watch your step
the floor is slippery.

Wooden doors then opened
to expose a large and well-stocked
kitchen boasting all the necessary

pans and gadgets.
Smell the spices and the fruits and
breads. We make our own of course.
This is a place for
tasting, feeling
warm and full and
satisfied. For sharing
meals and talk and
giving and receiving
sustenance.
And in those bottles?
Our own wine we mix.
Your bread and wine?
But not ours only. Wine and bread
become both blood and body
to instill the path of insight
into those who dare to enter this next room.

Floor to ceiling doors
cathedral shaped she opened
to admit us to a stone and glass roofed chapel
heavy with the mist of incense
and yet filled with sunlight falling
on the plainstone altar vacant
save for one small plate of bread
and common cup of wine - the table set.
Wisdom's voice was silenced as
her eyes whispered to mine:
This is the center of my house.
It is a room for kneeling
praying, supplicating and
remembering who we are.
It is a room for crying
out to God and for demanding
that the promises be kept.
It is a quiet place of deafening

silence where forgiveness found
is anger lost.
It is the central place of in-sight
from the co-creator Presence
that dwells here and in us always.
Wisdom's hand was warm in mine as
we walked touching holding leaving
through a cloistered hallway
wafting incense silently
behind us.

Many moments passed unbroken
by a word or gesture
even though we stood some time
surrounded by vast volumes
bound by leathersmell.
Then Wisdom spoke:
Libraries of written knowledge
different cultures thoughts and
feelings are recorded for
perusal here.
All the words proposals structures
brilliant remedies solutions sciences
theologies are represented in
this place.
Scanning all around I
wondered how it is with
all this knowledge we still live in threat of
war and famine.
Wisdom heard my thinking.
Well, said she,
If all it took to save the
world was intellect this
room could be much smaller. Also you will note
there are no windows here.
Knowledge by itself alone

unbalanced is not
wisdom.
Come, there are
yet two rooms you must see.

Muted coolsoft colors met
us as we entered a
room filled with one huge
bed and blankets pillows.
This place, she began,
I get the picture said
I smiling
Only part of it as usual
she corrected. Let
me finish. While of
course it is a place for
knowing intimately loving being
vulnerable, for sleeping
changing consciousness and leaving
what we call reality behind it is
a place for
dreaming.
White and black and multicolored
images of wishes fantasies of
beasts and evil good and
hopeful futurepast and
spirits holy and
redemptive.
Fear and love are
here as in the
other rooms I
said.
Wisdom replied: As
well as majesty and weakness
and the all-pervasive quality
so hidden or not obvious

in the other rooms but
blatant in this
next one.
I grasped Wisdom by
her forearm turned
her toward me
facing those deep eyes
and questioned
What is in that room?
She answered
her lips moving with a
soultouch stillness penetrating
deep within my
being. You
already know
that it
is
Death.

Eyelids closed and shaking
I let Wisdom lead
me through the last
door thinking horrors
would assault me surely
as I soon would breathe
my last.
Coming to a stop in
silence Wisdom let go of
my hand and offered these
words.
You may open now.
Squinting first in
fear then blinded by the
spacious light I
shouted chiding Wisdom
No! This is the living room where

we first started!
Yes, said she. It
is the dying
room as well. They
are the same.
Here just as before
the pulse of life
beats by the year and day
and minute. Here just as
before it is a room for
feeling crying laughing
warming growing
ending and beginning dying and
rebirth.

I began to
cry with tears of bitterness
and sorrow cleansing
healing scars too old and
deep to have been
touched before this moment.
Wisdom came to me and
held me and for
the first time I too
embraced her
held her
feared and loved and wanted
to stay with
her in her
seven gabled house.

Knowing, Wisdom parted yet
still holding each at arm's
length.
Said she: Wisdom kept inside is

wisdom wasted unacknowledged
barren boring and quickly
forgotten useless and
demeaning.
But to share all
this, I said, is to
risk confrontation worldly
judgment prejudice
and Yes said
she and
crucifixion.
And it is as you
have seen to also
take the risk of
healing, loving, holding,
risking resurrection.

Looking at her I
repeated my initial
greeting; It is
time, I said.
Perhaps it is said
she. I hope you'll come
and visit sometime in
the future when
we both have changed
again.
Nodding,
leaving, I reflected to
her that our meeting
and encounter had
been for me like a prayer.
Smiling,
leaving,
Wisdom said In that
case let us not end with

Good-bye but with
Amen.

Mark 11.1-11

And when they drew near to Jerusalem, to Bethphage and Bethany, at the Mount of Olives, he sent two of his disciples, and said to them, "Go into the village opposite you, and immediately as you enter it you will find a colt tied, on which no one has ever sat; untie it and bring it. If any one says to you, 'Why are you doing this?' say, 'The Lord has need of it and will send it back here immediately.'"

And they went away, and found a colt tied at the door out in the open street; and they untied it. And those who stood there said to them, "What are you doing, untying the colt?" And they told them what Jesus had said; and they let them go.

And they brought the colt to Jesus, and threw their garments on it; and he sat upon it. And many spread their garments on the road, and others spread leafy branches which they had cut from the fields. And those who went before and those who followed cried out, "Hosanna! Blessed is he who comes in the name of the Lord! Blessed is the kingdom of our father David that is coming! Hosanna in the highest."

And he entered Jerusalem, and went into the temple; and when he had looked round at everything, as it was already late, he went out to Bethany with the twelve.

Palm Reader

This letter may never be found. And if it is found, it may never be read. People may find it too personal, or too revealing, or too controversial. But I must write, even if the scroll falls to dust in the earthen jar in which I will store it, for it is written as much to myself as to Christians who will follow after me.

My name is Joel, though that is unimportant to you. My job is also not important to know, except to say I make the same kinds of decisions every day that you do. My decisions affect the lives of many people, my friends, my coworkers, my family, my community. They are important decisions to me, though they may not mean much in the grand scheme of things, and so I always like to engage in conversation with people to discover how they decide what to do.

It was with that goal in mind that I approached the man called Jesus this morning on the road to Jerusalem. I had been watching his band of followers for some time as they traveled. There seemed to be considerable arguing among them as to how to deal with what they called the Jerusalem problem.

Some thought this was the time to show their cards, mass their strength, and call on the will of the common people to bring in the new political kingdom of God. Others thought this was too volatile a moment, and, if they did, their movement would not only be set back, it would be crushed.

Throughout this discussion, Jesus appeared amazingly silent. I had heard about him through the rumours of his healing and preaching. And I must admit I was a bit disappointed when I saw his followers arguing and Jesus not doing anything about it.

They stopped for a while at the Mount of Olives. The arguing continued until I saw Jesus raise a hand. He said something to two of the disciples and they walked away into the village opposite us. The rest of them sat where they were and got out provisions to eat. Jesus, seemingly uninterested in *their* stomachs *or* his, walked away from them, near where I was standing, and muttered to himself.

"Why did I *do* that?" he asked, shaking his bearded head. "Why did I *do* that?"

I turned to him and said: "Why did you do *what*?"

Startled, Jesus looked at me. "What? Who are you?"

"Just an innocent bystander," I said.

"Well," he said, "maybe that's what I need is an innocent bystander." He pointed across the dusty road and pursed his lips. "I've got a bunch of bystanders over there, but they're a far cry from innocent."

He seemed lost in thought.

"So, uh, what is it you're wondering about?" I asked.

"Huh? Oh, yes. I was wondering why I did that." He pointed into the village.

"Did what?"

"Sent those two men into the village to get a colt for me."

"Well you must have had a reason."

"Of *course* I had a reason!" he bellowed. "I just don't know if I want to go through with it!"

"Through with what?"

His eyes pierced through me.

"Riding into Jerusalem."

The shocked look on my face must have been obvious.

"So you think I shouldn't do it either?"

"I.....I didn't say that."

"You didn't have to," he said. "Good. That's another vote on my side. Half the people huddled over there, people I've known for three years, traveled with, taught, learned from, laughed with, cried over - half of them think we should detour around the city; that the time is not right. And my best instincts agree with them."

"And the others?" I asked.

"They think a symbolic ride into Jerusalem will rally the people in their behalf, confront the authorities, bring about the power to overthrow oppression, end poverty, and free the people."

"And you disagree with that?"

"Yes." He looked at me with those piercing eyes again. "I disagree with them both," he said. "Neither one knows what power is. The one faction thinks power is strength, power is numbers, power is wealth and security and certainty. The other faction thinks power is found in always avoiding conflict, subjecting yourself to the authorities, giving in and giving up."

"And you? What do *you* think power is?"

"The only real power is found in risk, in vulnerability, in openness, in pouring yourself out." He looked at the ground. "And that is not what they want to hear."

"So, at the risk of being pushy..," I said. "...why *did* you send for the colt?"

"I don't *know*!" he said loudly. "I don't *know*! It was a stupid move." He paced in the dust. "I guess I was just buying time to decide. If I had my choice right this second I wouldn't do it. I wouldn't ride into Jerusalem." He stopped and looked at me. "And do you know why?"

I stood staring.

"Because I know what will happen if I do! At first all these adoring people will line the roads and shout their praises. Who knows, they may even throw down palm leaves as if honoring a king.

"They'll shout to me 'HOSANNA.' Do you know what HOSANNA means?"

I was so taken with his vehemence, I could not answer.

"It means 'O SAVE US.' But what happens when I take them seriously and respond to that cry? Then maybe they find out they really don't want to be saved so much. When people shout to me to help them, to save them, they usually have in mind specifically what they want me to do. But it almost *never* is what they need!

"And when I respond to their HOSANNA, take seriously their cry for healing, their cry for love, their cry for mercy and forgiveness - when I welcome their HOSANNA and come to them, suddenly their HOSANNA becomes CRUCIFY HIM, CRUCIFY HIM."

His face was flushed and sweating and his breath panting. I tried to break in with a comforting question. "But why...?"

"Because..." He stopped pacing and held me by the shoulders. "...don't you see? The ride into Jerusalem is not to win a popularity contest, or to get earthly power or wealth or pride."

He stared into my stolid face.

"The ride into Jerusalem is to go and overturn all the tables in the temple. It's not until all the comfortable tables are overturned that healing can take place, that HOSANNA can be accomplished. It is not until all the comfortable tables in people's lives are overturned, whether those tables represent religious beliefs, or social status, or cultural arrogance, or prejudicial pride, or whatever other idols we worship - not until they are overturned that healing can occur."

"I....understand," I said, slowly. "And...the price of that disruption is death - death of dreams, death of false hopes, death of idols, death of relationships...perhaps even your own personal death."

Jesus' wide eyes softened, and he nearly smiled.

"You...do...understand," he said.

I paused, then asked: "And what will happen if you do not get on that colt?"

"I don't know," he said, quietly. "God is always seeking after mankind. And whether it is through me or you or someone else in another century, God will continually break into the world for love and hope and forgiveness and peace."

"But it sounds like it doesn't matter if you do or don't. God will find another way if you decide not to."

"It's true God will find a way now and in the future." He folded his arms across his chest, as if cradling himself. "But this is something I've been struggling with my whole life. And it has finally come down to this decision."

He looked at me with a plaintive strength that held me spellbound.

"I don't want to die," he said. "But I know I will *whether or not* I get on that colt. We all will. I guess the question really is one of how we will live in the meantime."

He paused and looked down the road at the two men coming toward us. They were leading a brownish red colt on a short tether.

"I guess..." Jesus said, "...that I can trust that God will prevail whether I get on that colt and ride to the temple or send the animal back and go my own separate way."

"That's true," I said. "But sometimes God needs our decisions to help Him come into the world."

Jesus came to me and put his arms around me.

"Thank you," he said.

"You have made your decision then?" I said.

"No. Not yet. But you have helped."

He turned to walk back to the disciples who, now, were standing waiting for him. Then he turned back.

"What is your name?"

"Joel."

He smiled. "Thank you, Joel."

I watched as the colt was led closer and closer to him. Suddenly, Jesus raised his hand and the two men stopped, about twenty feet from the crowd. My heart raced in my chest, as I saw him turn around and walk the other way.

Then, somewhere on the edge of the crowd, a small child cried.

Jesus stopped, and turned his head toward the sound. He saw the child and went to her, picked her up in his arms and held her close until she stopped. It was as though, in that moment, he had the entire universe in his roughened hands.

He looked at the crowd, and looked at the child. Then he kissed her on the forehead and handed her back to her grateful father.

Then, and I must admit I was in tears myself at this point, Jesus walked back across the dusty road in front of the disciples and slung a leg over the back of that colt.

Mine were the first eyes he saw as he turned toward Jerusalem.

I am writing this letter on the same day he entered the temple and cleared it and healed those who came to him. I do not know what will happen next. I do know I will follow him forever. I will live my life by his precepts, choosing risk, choosing to be vulnerable, choosing the right rather than the easy or comfortable, choosing life with him even though it means death of one kind or another.

The decision for him was not easy. No decision for God ever is. But I learned from this Jesus that God needs us to make those decisions if God is to come into the world to answer our cry of HOSANNA.

I, Joel, write this with my own hand. May you who read this and you who hear it have the love to decide as Jesus did when your colt is led up to you.

Acts 16.16-34

As we were going to the place of prayer, we were met by a slave girl who had a spirit of divination and brought her owners much gain by soothsaying. She followed Paul and us, crying, "These men are servants of the Most High God, who proclaim to you the way of salvation." And this she did for many days. But Paul was annoyed, and turned and said to the spirit, "I charge you in the name of Jesus Christ to come out of her." And it came out that very hour.

But when her owners saw that their hope of gain was gone, they seized Paul and Silas and dragged them into the market place before the rulers; and when they had brought them to the magistrates they said, "These men are Jews and they are disturbing our city. They advocate customs which it is not lawful for us Romans to accept or practice." The crowd joined in attacking them; and the magistrates tore the garments off them and gave orders to beat them with rods. And when they had inflicted many blows upon them, they threw them into prison, charging the jailer to keep them safely. Having received this charge, he put them into the inner prison and fastened their feet in the stocks.

But about midnight Paul and Silas were praying and singing hymns to God, and the prisoners were listening to them, and suddenly there was a great earthquake, so that the foundations of the prison were shaken; and immediately all the doors were opened and every one's fetters were unfastened. When the jailer woke and saw that the prison doors were open, he drew his sword and was about to kill himself, supposing that the prisoners had escaped.

But Paul cried with a loud voice, "Do not harm yourself, for we are all here." And he called for lights and rushed in, and trembling with fear he fell down before Paul and Silas, and brought them out and said, "Men, what must I do to be saved?" And they said, "Believe in the Lord Jesus, and you will be saved, you and your household."

And they spoke the word of the Lord to him and to all that were in his house. And he took them the same hour of the night, and washed their wounds, and he was baptized at once, with all his family. Then he brought them up into his house, and set food before them; and he rejoiced with all his household that he had believed in God.

Letter from Prison

This is perhaps the last letter I shall ever write. It is written not just for my personal family but for my Christian family. It is also written for myself. I hope that if I set the details down before me I will be better able to make some sense of them. Maybe not, but let us see.

My name is Paulus; ironically the same name as the one I was told to guard. I've been a jailer at this prison for 15 years. In here you get the straight rap on people, not just the usual gossip from the streets but the stories from those who are out there, involved in the crimes. That's how I knew about Paul and Silas before I ever laid eyes on them.

The two had been under suspicion for some time. They were constantly stirring people up just by their presence; and when they spoke they seemed to go against all our customs and laws. The rulers had kept a close eye on them, even infiltrated their group to learn more, so it was no surprise when this latest incident happened.

It seems Paul had gotten tired of that slave girl chasing him around with her spirit shouting at him. In a typical fit of anger he called the spirit out of her, thereby not only depriving her owners of some substantial income, but also depriving the girl of her considerable notoriety and popularity. It was not a very nice thing to do. But you know how Paul is.

Anyway, it seems that was the last straw. They were arrested, stripped, beaten worse than those I usually see here, and sent to me to guard safely until some final disposition could be made. Because I knew a promotion was in store if I did the job well, I put them into the inner prison and locked their feet in the stocks. Since their hands were also tightly tied you might say they were heavily invested in stocks and bonds. Or you might not. It is important not to lose you sense of humour in this place.

Hard as I tried I couldn't get to sleep for the racket those two made praying out loud and singing at the top of their lungs. It wouldn't have been so bad but Paul sings like he writes. And Silas has a voice like a bird - a vulture. I had had enough of their screeching and was just getting up to go yell at them again when I stumbled over my chair and fell into the table. I thought I had just lost my balance but quickly realized that every stone in the prison was shaking and cracking from a severe earthquake.

I shook my head so as not to pass out and noticed that cell doors were opening and prisoners were getting loose. I knew that if the two I was guarding got free I would suffer a fate worse than theirs. My reputation would be blemished, my career over, and by law I would receive the punishment meant for them. There was only one way to save face. I drew my sword and was about to plunge it into my gut when I heard Paul calling to me. "Don't harm yourself," he said, "for we are all here."

I don't know if I was more frightened from the earthquake or from facing my own death. I know I was grateful for having survived both. I could hardly believe the words coming out of my rather cynical, inured mouth, as I fell down in front of them there by the torchlight in the cell. I think with the tip of the sword at my belly I flashed through my life and didn't see much of real value or purpose. I think most people do that - wait until the sword is at their belly to evaluate who and where they are. Then it was as though Paul called me out of death.

I asked him what I had to do to be saved - saved from boredom, saved from the demands and customs of my society, saved from the mediocrity of my life, saved from the creeping conformity of my world, saved from my images, saved from my fears and hopes, saved from myself.

His answer sounded too simple - and it was. He said "Believe...." What he meant was "listen," "embrace," "repent," "forgive," "accept," "submit," "demand," "proclaim," "commit." I was so hungry for these words that we seemed to talk, to argue, to question, to hear The Story over and over again forever. It was in fact but hours - and it was at *my* house where I could wash their wounds, feed them, save them as they cleansed me and my family, fed us with the Spirit, saved us with our God.

I was disappointed at first when they left. Life went on pretty much the way it had for us. I went to work; my wife and kids led their lives the same way; people were not much different. But then gradually, and especially in communion with other members of The Way, we began to see things differently, to hear things differently, to do things differently. And our former friends began to see us as somehow changed, no longer worshiping the same societal gods, goals, customs. Just like Jesus, we became a threat. I suppose Christians, those who take seriously their beliefs, will always be a threat to the status quo, for ours is a revolutionary ethic.

About a week ago we were meeting in my home, celebrating the Lord's Supper when the inevitable knock occurred a the door. Now the keeper has become the kept. Now it is I who have been beaten. Now it is I who am heavily invested in stocks and bonds. Now it is my own vulture voice that sings and prays aloud in this dank inner prison cell. But no earthquake comes.

Oh, I knew when I chose to follow Jesus it could go either way. Being a Christian is no guarantee life will go well; but it's no guarantee life will go poorly either. Maybe it is possible to live in this society and compromise beliefs. It was not for me. And I wonder about those after me. What issues will they face? Will they have weapons to destroy the world? Will they have medicines to prolong life and cheat death? Will their scientists have means to create life itself? What will Christians do about those things? Will they do what I am doing now?

I know where this will lead. And still I would follow again. Not because of the earthquake, not because of Paul and Silas, not even because of my Christian community; but because I know that the Way of Christ Jesus is right.

I hear them coming for me now. I have worked in this place long enough to know what coming at this hour and with so many voices has to mean. So I must end this letter from prison. I will fold it and hide it, hoping that someone from The Way will find and read and keep and pass it on; hoping that someone, maybe centuries from now, will hear and grow, be strengthened to continue the revolutionary bringing in of God's kingdom through these meager words of Paulus.

Thanks be to God. Amen.

Mark 4.35-41, 5.1-20

They came to the other side of the sea, to the country of the Gerasenes. And when he had come out of the boat, there met him out of the tombs a man with an unclean spirit, who lived among the tombs; and no one could bind him any more, even with a chain; for he had often been bound with fetters and chains, but the chains he wrenched apart, and the fetters he broke in pieces; and no one had the strength to subdue him. Night and day among the tombs and on the mountains he was always crying out, and bruising himself with stones.

And when he saw Jesus from afar, he ran and worshipped him; and crying out with a loud voice, he said," What have you to do with me, Jesus, Son of the Most High God: I adjure you by God, do not torment me." For he had said to him, "Come out of the man, you unclean spirit!"

And Jesus asked him "What is your name?" He replied,"My name is Legion; for we are many." And he begged him eagerly not to send them out of the country.

Now a great herd of swine was feeding there on the hillside; and they begged him, "Send us to the swine, let us enter them. So he gave them leave. And the unclean spirits came out, and entered the swine; and the herd, numbering about two thousand, rushed down the steep bank into the sea, and were drowned in the sea.

The herdsmen fled, and told it in the city and in the country. And people came to see what it was that had happened. And they came to Jesus, and saw the demoniac sitting there, clothed and in his right mind, the man who had had the legion; and they were afraid.

And those who had seen it told what had happened to the demoniac and to the swine. And they began to beg Jesus to depart from their neighborhood.

And as he was getting into the boat, the man who had been possessed with demons begged him that he might be with him. But he refused, and said to him, "Go home to your friends, and tell them how much the Lord as done for you, and how he has had mercy on you." And he went away and began to proclaim in the Decapolis how much Jesus had done for him; and all men marveled.

A Man's Best Friend
Is His Demon

AAAAAAARRRRRRRRGGGGGGGGHHHHHHHHH!!!!!!!!

Will you be quiet?

NO!! NOT UNTIL YOU LEAVE ME ALONE!!!

Oh, not THAT again. When are you gonna get the POINT, dummy? I'm here for LIFE.

Your's or mine?

Yes.

Swell. Doesn't seem like much of a life to ME. You drag me in and out of these smelly tombs full of dead rotting bodies...

So I like company...

And your presence makes me so mad I SCREAM all the time....

I like a little background noise, don't you?

...so that people try to bind me with ropes and chains to calm me down.

And don't me and the rest of the Legionairres always bust you out, Big Boy? Where do you think all your STRENGTH comes from? It certainly isn't just within YOU! What an INGRATE!! The least you could do is to wear our hat!

But you're so....so....UNCLEAN!! Do you know that before I met you I wore a tie and clean underwear every day?

Yeah, and it's a wonder they didn't fire you for coming to work like that. Didn't you ever hear of CLOTHES?

You know what I mean, smart face. I mean I had a good job. I was respected in the community. People knew my name. I had a future to look forward to. Now what do I do? One look at you and I smash myself in the face with rocks. Maybe if I make myself less attractive you'll all go away. Maybe if I call enough attention somebody will come and send you away.

Send us away? AWAY??? YOU were the one who invited us IN, if you'll use that pimple of gray matter you call a brain and remember right. YOU were the one who attracted US - and NOW you want to get rid of us? Not on you life!!

AAAAAAAARRRRRRRRRRGGGGGGGGGGHHHHHHHHHH!!!!!

A little louder, if you please. We like it when you do that REAL loud when you hit yourself with stones. We Legionairres are into hard rock.

Just leave me alone.

What are you complaining about? You've got everything you ever wanted! You're WELL known in the community. Everybody knows YOUR name! You've got a great job entertaining everyone and giving people something to talk about. And how many other people do you know who get to go around smelling like you do, screaming at the top of their lungs and complaining about demons nobody but you can see? What FREEDOM!

FREEDOM?? This is pure slavery!

Yeah. Ain't love wonderful? We all get along so well. We play and you suffer. We provide your notoriety! We provide your strength! You just provide the room and board. Not a bad bargain - and remember, you DID ask us in. You wouldn't know what to do WITHOUT us now.

Hey, who's that over there?

The Boat Boy? He's nobody important. Forget about him. Here, have some rocks.

I heard someone say it's JESUS! I've heard about him. I'll bet HE can help me! (starts to go.)

Yeah, sure. That's what you said about US, too.

(stops short) Hmmmm. Maybe you're right.

Of COURSE we're right. If you let HIM in, there's no telling WHAT would happen to you.

Yeah. It's probably safer to...

Sure it is. You stay here with us where it's safe and sound and...

WAIT a minute!! What am I SAYING?? Why am I LISTENING to you?

Because you know we're RIGHT, old pal. If you swap us out for that Jesus Spirit you'll REALLY be in hot water. You won't HAVE to hit yourself with stones, stupid, 'cause other people will do it FOR you. At least with US people know what to EXPECT from you. If you let HIM in you'll be going against their social expectations and even their religious customs. You'll start talking about REALLY crazy things like peace and feeding people and protecting the poor and divesting South African stocks and selling the nuke and limiting building heights. You might even want the charismatics and the conservatives to sit down and talk theology!! You'll rock that dingy out there and they'll dump you in the sea so fast you won't have time to learn the backstroke!!

(thoughtfully) Yeah....but did you SEE what he did to the WATER?

All done with lights and mirrors, friend. An illusion. We could do that too if we wanted to. Don't be conned by him.

You're probably right...........but I couldn't do much WORSE than I am now with you characters.

Oh yes you could. If we leave, you'll probably just be taken over by some... FOREIGN legion....

But even if I did I still think...

Don't DO it!!!

(waves) Hey!!!! J-E-S-U-S!!! Over HERE!

NOW you've done it. Here he comes. Oh well, no biggie. We'll just talk to him and send him on his way, right guys?

Now be nice.

NICE!...NICE!! Are you kidding?? THIS guy wants our JOB!! Did you HEAR what he SAID to us??? He said to 'COME OUT.' (speaking to Jesus) Now wait just a minute here. What have YOU to do with US, Jesus, Son of the Most High God? I beg you, by that same God, do not torment me!" (speaking to others) Okay, THAT showed him!

Yeah, I can see he's really scared. Go ahead, answer him.

Answer him WHAT?

He ASKED you your NAME!

Name, huh. Well...uh...okay. My name is LEGION; for we are MANY.

Did you hear that?

Hear what? I didn't hear anything. Did you guys hear anything? No, they didn't hear anything either.

He said it's okay for you to go.

It's....it's....OKAY for us...it's O-KAY for us to....to....GO?

Uh-huh. He said we'd served each other well up until now. You got what you needed from me and I got what I needed from you. But I don't need OR WANT that any more.

Oh yeah, sure. Turn your back on your best friend. After all this time we've been together. Best relationship we've had in years and now, on a complete whim, you decide you've outgrown us. Thanks a lot, nice guy. You too, Jesus.

I really would like to part as friends.

FRIENDS?? FRIENDS?? Some kind of friend YOU are. YOU go off with HIM and what are WE left with? A PIG in a POKE - THAT'S what!

I just want you to know that it's sad seeing you go. And scary, and uncomfortable.

Well it's a mixed bag being released from you, too, you know. You were just as much of a prison for us as we were for you.

That's a surprise to me. So it looks like we're both getting our freedom.

Yeah, that's the way it looks. But I've got a feeling we'll be employed again, real soon.

Where will you go?

We're negotiating that right now. (to Jesus) You know, Jesus, the way this guy smells, those pigs would be a step UP.

He said you're free to go.

We know. (smiling) And we ALSO know that you're BOTH gonna be REAL sorry we left.

Well, goodbye anyway.

Bye, sucker. You two are a LOT dumber than we thought. Watch THIS!!

(exits)

AAAAAAAARRRRRRRRRGGGGGGGGGHHHHHHHHHHH!!!! *OH* THAT HURT!!! Holy Moses!!!...oh, uh, no offense, Jesus. But will you LOOK at those PIGS!! They're all heading into the........uh....oh..... Uh, Jesus, I think I'll just mosey back into that cave a while if you don't mind.

I do feel better. I have washed and put on my clean clothes, my tie and clean underwear feel especially good. Here are the herdsmen back from the town with the authorities to look at me. They point and stare at me, even more than they did before. They don't know what to think.

Some people are saying I'll never change. They don't want me to change. They were more comfortable with me doing that other stuff than they are seeing me sitting here like this with my senses about me. They could handle me then. They thought they were better than I was - or at least a lot different. Now they're wondering what would happen if they gave up THEIR demons - and they're scared. They don't know how to deal with me now. I wonder if they're right about my turning back and wanting the demons to return...I wonder if...

Now they're pointing at me and telling Jesus to get out of the neighborhood. They're shouting at him, saying he has no sense of priorities. Doesn't he understand trickle down economics? Doesn't he understand they'd rather have a raving crazy person and some nice fat hogs than peace and healing and a lousy economy?

He's heading back for the boat. I have to catch him and go with him. He could use a strong, clear headed person like me to handle crowds like this. Why, if they got out of hand there's no telling...

Say, Jesus...could I ask you a.... What do you mean...'Go home to my friends?' The only friends I've had for YEARS have been those demons. And now THEY'RE gone...and now YOU'RE going to leave me too!! The demons were RIGHT!! I'm going to be left all ALONE! What do you mean I DO have friends here? Not after what happened to those PIGS I don't!...What kind of friends?... Others...other followers of yours? How will I know them?... I'll know them by their behavior... Swell, I'll go out and look for some people who frequently fly in the face of social propriety, constantly question the status quo and aren't afraid of other people's demons. That shouldn't be too hard to spot.

Okay, okay. I'll go tell them what happened to me - what I did and you did and we did.

Just do me a favor, will you?

Be careful crossing the lake in that boat.

Oh, and Jesus?

Thanks.

(A few moments of silence pass as the person watches Jesus leave. Then, from out of nowhere, comes a yell....)

You'll want us BACK, you know. They ALWAYS do. It's just a matter of TIME. Remember - A MAN'S BEST FRIEND IS HIS DEMON.

Luke 17.11-19

On the way to Jerusalem he was passing along between Samaria and Galilee. And as he entered a village, he was met by ten lepers, who stood at a distance and lifted up their voices and said, "Jesus, Master, have mercy on us." When he saw them he said to them, "Go and show yourselves to the priests." And as they went they were cleansed. Then one of them, when he saw that he was healed, turned back, praising God with a loud voice: and he fell on his face at Jesus' feet, giving him thanks. Now he was a Samaritan.

Then said Jesus, "Were not ten cleansed? Where are the nine? Was no one found to return and give praise to God except this foreigner?" And he said to him, "Rise and go your way; your faith has made you well."

Leper Letter

(One night, as I was preparing some background material for a story, I decided to search out information in the basement of the seminary library. After I had been there about an hour, poring over huge tomes of Biblical commentary, I fell into a deep sleep and dreamed a strange dream. In the dream there was an ancient door behind one of the basement bookshelves. Behind that door were some archeological remnants being stored until they could be examined by learned scholars in coming years.

I awoke rather suddenly and, as if still in the dream, went looking for that door. To my surprise, I found the dust covered bookshelf way back in a dark, forgotten corner of the basement. Carefully moving it aside, I found the door, nearly hidden by years of cobwebs, dust, and decay. My heart beat wildly as I slowly turned the knob and opened the door. My squinting eyes reluctantly adjusted to the darkness, and I saw before me a collection of implements and items which had obviously come from an ancient dig. Almost without my control, my arm reached out for a particular item right in front: a parchment scroll, tied with a bit of dried, faded cloth. It was as though it had been left there for me to find, and so I gently untied the knot and opened the scroll. I read a few lines, then brought it out into the dim, basement light, and set out to translate it.

It was a letter from the leper. It is called the Christopholus Scroll.)

The Christopholus Scroll

I am about to die. That may sound somewhat dramatic to you, whoever you are, as I imagine you who will find this scroll will be reading it in a safe, perhaps even comfortable place. But for me, death has been a fact of life for many years.

I am a leper. But before you throw down this manuscript and burn it for fear of contamination, let me hasten to assure you that I am not dying of leprosy. Not any more. I was healed of the leprosy by my interaction with a certain Jesus of Nazareth many years ago. I am dying because the residual effects of the disease have taken their toll. I am weak. My body is worn out. I am tired. I am ready to die. But before I do I want to set down as clearly as I can what happened that day on the Jerusalem road. It was a minor event in the history of the world. I am sure it has gone unnoticed. The prophet's name will probably not survive him or me, there are so many of them these days; unless of course he is who people say he is.

My name, though insignificant to you now, is Christopholus. At one time I was a successful businessman in a city near Samaria. The details are not important. Suffice it to say I had a very profitable service and a well run organization. I had a lovely wife and two fine children with another one on the way. Things were going well for me and my family and our extended families. Then I got sick. At first we thought it was some minor ailment, but then the physicians, shaking their heads in disbelief, told me it was leprosy.

My life disintegrated just as quickly as my body itself rotted from within and began to decay. I was made to leave the city and to go to live in a leper colony. My clothes were burned. My possessions were buried. I was a disgrace to my community. To my family it was as though I were dead. And I was dead to myself also; hopeless, despairing, angry, depressed, confused. I prayed to the capricious gods who had struck me with this misfortune and begged them to continue their folly, to kill me, to let me die quickly instead of painfully watching myself die a piece at a time. They would not listen, but their folly did continue. Within the colony I was the only Samaritan. My gods were not their gods, my ways not their ways. I was an outcast among outcasts. Death was a welcome friend who ignored me like everyone else did for years and years and years.

One hot day ten of us were sitting beside the road to Jerusalem, begging. It was a busy highway with many people traveling to and from the great city with news and, even better for us, with food and money. We were taunted and ignored and only occasionally noticed by someone feeling guilty or frightened or compassionate. We heard some commotion and rose as a group to see who it might be. We were used to soothsayers and prophets and magicians and healers coming down the road. They were all out to win followers and make money. Sometimes they promised to heal us; sometimes they just pointed to us as examples of sin; always they wanted to use us.

We overheard some of the normal people talking about what this prophet had done elsewhere, and so we went up to him. We kept our required distance, so as not to offend or infect him. Respectfully, and out of hope, we called to him from the far edge of the crowd. We called to him: 'Jesus, Master, have mercy on us.'

Surprisingly, he heard us and stopped. I was stunned. I felt nauseous. Looking into his eyes was the most comforting and frightening experience in my life. I knew in that moment that my life could change. And, this is very hard to admit, I was not sure I wanted it to. As accustomed as I had been to being a successful person, now I had become accustomed to being a leper. I lived in expectation of death. I watched the days go by with excruciating slowness. I had an image of myself as a leper, and accepted other people's image of me in that role also.

I did not know what would happen if I would be healed. I would have to give up the leprosy, and yet live with the stigma of it, the scars of it, the reputation of it for the rest of my life. I would no longer have the excuse of leprosy to define my identity and to avoid responsibility for my life. Maybe it was just easier to turn around, to go away from this Jesus, to ignore his healing, to continue to live up to my old image and to the demands of the crowd around me, sick and normal people, to remain a leper and to die a leper.

I looked down at the ground, down at my filthy rags and rotting skin. Then I looked back at him. Here was the first prophet who had taken us seriously. Rather than answer our shallow plea for mercy with money or food, this Jesus stopped and looked at us - and he gave us his time, his attention, his strength, his creating love. He silenced the crowd and walked over towards us. Not to offend or frighten us, he stood at a little distance. Then he spoke.

At first I didn't get it. I didn't understand him. Go and show ourselves to the priests? What good would that do? They don't want to see us. I thought this Jesus was just another charlatan and I turned to go away as did all the others. Once again I had been disappointed, but I was also relieved. I could keep the old identity. I would not have to accept the responsibility that came with change, or deal with the anger and disappointment of those who were so invested in my being a leper. And yet, I thought. And yet there was something in his eyes.

It was as though he saw through me, or inside me, or maybe it was beyond me. Yes, that was it. He saw beyond me, beyond my leprosy, beyond my fear, beyond my pain and wish for death. The image of myself I saw reflected in his eyes was one of wholeness, integration;

it was clean, clear, forceful, self respecting, healed. And that spark from him touched the spark in me and ignited. I could not stop it, regardless of my fears, regardless of what others might want or say. I decided to take the risk of accepting what I saw in his eyes, to take the risk of further rejection, to take the risk of further failure, to take the risk of giving up my old identity - to take the risk of healing.

At the moment I made the decision, I started breathing more heavily, but the breaths were deeper, not panicky, but relaxed; more relaxed than I had been able to breathe for years. I felt different, relieved; and I also felt something I had not felt for a long, long, time. It was such a strange feeling that it took me a second or two to identify it. I felt hopeful.

I did not notice the change at first. One of the crowd of normal people pointed at me, and then at all of us. I am used to being pointed at, but not in that way. The people looked astonished, even frightened.

It was then that I looked at my hands. I held them up in front of my face and could not believe what I saw. They were smooth and pulsing with life.They were whole! They looked just like normal hands - like yours, for instance. I clasped them to my face and it felt like they looked - smooth and whole. My fingers felt the damp tears flowing down over my cheeks. I fell to my knees and sobbed.

It seemed like an eternity, though I am sure it was only a few seconds, until I found my voice again. I looked up into the sky and lifted my newly strong arms and thanked whatever god had done this for me, or was it with me? Then, as if a chill went through my new body, I knew which God it was. It was the God represented in that Jesus person, the one with the eyes that saw beyond. Then I stood and turned around and walked back to him.

I fell to the ground in front of him in gratitude, but he lifted me up to stand face to face with him. When he saw my skin color, and my obvious Samaritan features he looked shocked. Where were the other nine? he asked. Why was it that this foreigner, myself, had been the only one to return to give thanks to God? I could see the hurt and disappointment, and even the anger in his eyes, those deep eyes again.

Then he said a strange thing. Unlike all the other prophets that have come down this road, he did not want me to follow him. He said to go *my* way, my own way from now on. Not his way, or the way of the crowd around me, or the world's way, or the way of my former lives, but *my* way now. And I knew I would have to find out what way that would be for me.

His eyes spoke once again when he said "Your faith has made you well." But he was wrong about that. It was not my faith alone that produced this change in me. It was his faith, his vision, combined with mine, our two sparks kindling each other that melted my former life and allowed me to emerge as I have been since that time.

I understand that he went on to Jerusalem and that he himself died there; was crucified, actually. I am telling you this because you may not have heard it, this is such an obscure part of the world. His followers say that he rose again somehow, that he died and is alive still. That does not surprise me. If he could do it with me, he certainly could do it with others and the God he represented could surely do it with him. I have known this resurrection myself thanks to him. And that is also why I write this with my waning strength. I want you to know it too.

For I have learned in these many years since that day that there is a part of each of us that is a leper, an outcast; an unwanted, unknown, frightening and irreconcilable part of us. That part may be due to a change in identity due to a loss, a death of a loved one, an illness or loss of ability due to circumstance or accident; it could be the part of us that is aging, growing up or growing old, the part that is the leper due to divorce, separation, alienation or despair; or the part that is alcoholic, mentally ill, prejudiced, status seeking, old, sick, or irresponsible. I wonder what the leprosy of your age will be?

In any case, it is to that part of you specifically that Jesus comes now - and offers a choice. You can hang on to the leprosy, keep that identity, live up to it every day for the rest of your life and continue to nurture it as it eats at you from within. Or you can let Jesus touch you with his eyes, let his spark touch your spark and watch what occurs. Others may not like it. No, others will not like it, you can be sure. They are comfortable with your leprosy. They know who you are, what you are about that way. And they fear that if change is possible for you, it might also be possible for them. You may not like the change for the same reasons. Your leprosy may be tough to live without. But you must choose. Not to decide is to decide.

I am feeling very weak now, and so I must close this tome. Although the disease is gone, I still suffer its effects, and that is understandable. One last thing though, before I put down my quill. If you do choose to accept the healing of your leper self, to let your faith and Jesus' faith make you whole, please remember to turn around and say thank you to the God he represents.

It is probably still true that foreigners, those outside the body of the allegedly faithful, are the ones who praise God most loudly and often. Those insiders - and I include myself among them now as I have become a Christian and have taken on a Christian name - those of us insiders tend to take him for granted, think that he does not need our gratefulness or does not want it, that it is somehow impolite to thank him, or awkward, or admitting of our need for help.

But I was there. I saw what it did for him, and I know also what it did for me. So remember, please remember, to turn around and face him, look at him and say directly to him how surprised and thankful you are. It will make a difference in his face and in his eyes. And it will make a difference in your life as well.

I, Christopholus, write this with my own hand. May you who find this scroll and all who read it come to know this obscure Jesus. And may the leper in you know healing with him this very day, and turn around.

Luke 7.11-17

Soon after healing the centurion's slave, Jesus went to a city called Nain, and his disciples and a great crowd went with him. As he drew near to the gate of the city, behold, a man who had died was being carried out, the only son of his mother, and she was a widow; and a large crowd from the city was with her.

And when the Lord saw her, he had compassion on her and said to her, "Do not weep." And he came and touched the bier, and the bearers stood still. And he said, "Young man, I say to you, arise." And the dead man sat up, and began to speak. And he gave him to his mother.

Fear seized them all; and they glorified God, saying, "A great prophet has arisen among us!" and "God has visited his people!" And this report concerning him spread through the whole of Judea and all the surrounding country.

Letter from Nain

My son is dead.

But that is not the end of the story.

I am not writing this. I cannot write. But it is important to set down what has happened for others to hear, so a friend who has practiced her letters secretly has agreed to put it down for me as I say it. For that, I owe her a debt I can never repay. Hopefully, the debt will repay itself, as those who read this in later times will learn from my story.

My name is not important, nor the name of my family. What is important for you to know is that I was born in this town of Nain, grew up here, married here and gave birth here. I am certain I will also die here. This is my home, and the home of my people for generations.

And you should know that my husband died when our son was two years old. That was fifteen years ago. It was a tragic disease, and even though they are so common here, he was the love of my life and I was devastated at his sudden death. The only thing that kept me going was the knowledge that the life of our son was now entirely in my hands.

I had to go on. I did not have the luxury of grieving for my husband for very long. My screaming two year old demanded every bit of time I had to spare - and more.

But I did it. With the help of my friends, I raised up a strong and handsome and healthy and knowledge-able son who was just like his father in so many ways. He made me proud of him. He worked hard and took care of us, just as his father had done before him. In fact, when he turned seventeen, just a few weeks ago, he began telling me I should not work so hard, I should take it easier, I should rest more and let him be respon-sible for more of the daily chores. And I had just about come to believe him when it happened.

They came and got me from the field where he worked that morning. They were in tears and I knew something terrible had befallen my only son, my only reminder of my husband, my only reason for living.

I ran to where he was and cradled his limp body in my arms. We still do not know what it was. He was stricken suddenly in the heat of the day. Someone saw him grab at his chest and then fall backward, hitting his head on a rock. And he breathed no more. He was dead.

And so was I.

The very next morning, we took him outside the city to bury his body. I could hardly walk in the funeral procession, I was so overcome with grief. Many people crowded around me, wailing as loud as I did, holding me up with their strong hands of comfort and sympathy. Because my son was so well known and loved, nearly the whole village was there.

No sooner had we passed through the gate of the city than we saw in the distance a man who was also being followed by a large crowd. I do not quite know how this happened, but I looked up and suddenly the man was standing there in front of me, with his many people looking on.

I thought this a strange sight, and rather rude at that, this intrusion into my private grief and the sorrow of our village. But, when I looked into the man's eyes, I felt his compassion and saw the tears of sadness welling up in him, though his words to me were "Do not weep." And I could not protest his wishes.

I could not even halt him when he commanded - and that is the word for it - he *commanded* the funeral bier to be let down before him. The bearers stood still and I nodded to them. Then the most extraordinary thing happened. It is so strange that you may not believe it - but I was there and it is my son I am telling you about - so I beg you to imagine this with me.

This man, this stranger who came up to our funeral and took charge and was not afraid of death or grief or numbers of the crowd or what anyone might think, this man who cut through all of the ceremony and all of our social customs, this man then came up and looked at my son and said: 'Young man, *I* say to you, arise.'

Well, I was stunned. And my surprise was not so much about what he said. No. It was the *way* he said it. It was as though he said - 'I know what all these people are saying about you; they are saying that you are dead, that there is no life in you, that the only thing to do is to weep and bury your body and leave you outside the walls, never again to return. But,' this man said to my son with power and authority, '*I* say to you *arise*. *I* say to you that there is life in you, that you are loved, accepted, forgiven, and commanded to use that life in you, and that love in you, to continue to serve and to share the talents you have been given.'

And then - please bear with me as I describe this to you - then my son stirred, and sat up on the pallet, and spoke. I could barely hear him, but I am certain his first words were - 'I choose life.'

Then the man took my son's hand and gave him back to me.

The crowd of my friends from our village was terrified - but so was the crowd following him. It was as though they saw themselves in my son - it was as though they were terrified that they were faced with the same exact choice somehow - the choice to listen to those who had them categorized, those who had them labeled, those who wanted them to remain in their places, to never change, to stay as they were to reassure a family structure, or an image, or a way of relating. And here this man comes along and says to them, just as he did to my son - *I* say to you - *arise*. Move on. Change. Grow. Mature. Commit. Let go. Trust me. Follow *my* image of you. Awake from your dead state and live again. Make the choice of life, or be dead forever.

And so fear seized them all.

But then they heeded his words and began to glorify God - not this man, mind you, but God, saying 'A great prophet has arisen among us!' and 'God has visited his people!' They saw in this man's works the presence of God and knew enough not to give the man the credit, but to glorify the One whom he represented, and to spread this report through the whole of Judea and the surrounding country.

And then he left - and the crowd of followers with him, including a few more from our village.

I still to not know the man's name. I heard from someone it was rumoured to be that Jesus whose name has been so associated with rebellion and new ideas and strange happenings. It does not matter to me. I know that my son was dead and that this man spoke to him and he was alive again. And that that is both terrifying and excitingly hopeful. It is terrifying because this same man talks to us all with the same message of choice. We can listen to him, or we can listen to the crowd around us. And it is hopeful because if we choose to follow him into life, we do it forever.

Even if we die.

And that is exactly what happened. Two months later my friends again ran to my house. And again I ran to my stricken son's side. Again I heard the story of how he clutched his chest and collapsed in the dirt. Again I held his head and watched him die. And I wept and mourned his death, as I did before, when we took him outside the village to bury his body in the earth.

But this time it was different. The encounter with that man, that Jesus man, did not make my grief any less this time, nor does it soften the blow of my son's loss, or fill the empty space in this vacant household, or heal the gaping hole in my heart. For my son is still dead. But the encounter with that man, that Jesus man, does tell me I will live again, if I choose; we will live again if we choose to risk it in front of the crowd and God and everyone.

I am exhausted now. But I feel better for having told someone, anyone; for having told you, so that, when this man comes into your life or your death, redefining what everyone else sees, reframing the meaning of what you and others have so long taken for granted, you may now also choose.

Because come he will.

Come he must.

Come he is destined by God to do.

My son is dead.

But that is not the end of the story.

Matthew 22.35-40

When the Pharisees heard that he had silenced the Sadducees, they gathered together, and one of them, a lawyer, asked him a question to test him. "Teacher, which commandment in the law is the greatest?"

He said to him "'You shall love the Lord you God with all you heart, and with all your soul, and with all your mind.' This is the first and great commandment. And a second is like it: 'You shall love your neighbor as yourself.' On these two commandments hang all the law and the prophets."

The Lawyer's Confession

I must write this journal entry in secret. I am a well known and respected member of the Pharisees. I have even been privy to the workings of the Sanhedrin from time to time. I have practiced as a lawyer in this city for thirty years and I am counted on for advice and counsel. So I cannot share my thoughts in public. They would be too devastating if they were known.

About mid morning today I was chatting with my friends when we got word that the person known as Jesus was approaching. We had heard how he had gotten the best of the Sadducees, and so a group of the Pharisees thought this would be a good time to put him to the test. They wanted me to be their spokesperson, and whispered to me what to say to him.

I must admit, when I first saw him, I was not impressed. He looked much like every other religious fanatic I had seen. Same clothes, same group of disciples and stragglers around him, everybody wanting something from him. I actually felt kind of sorry for the man.

But then he spoke.

His voice had a power I had never heard before. There was authority in it, and, at the same time, vulnerability and love.

I hesitated a moment, suddenly not sure I wanted to go through with this. It was as though I were caught in a dream, not able to stop the words coming out of my mouth, yet fearful of where they might lead. As I spoke the words to catch him, I knew it was myself who was about to be put to the test.

'There are 613 commandments, 365 negative and 248 positive,' I told him. 'Which of these is the greatest?'

He thought for a moment, and scanned his piercing eyes around the crowd. I was certain he would not know what to say. Then he answered, 'You shall love the Lord your God with all your heart, and with all your soul, and with all your mind. This is the great and first commandment. And a second is like it: You shall love your neighbor as yourself. On these two commandments depend all the law and the prophets.'

Well, even the least learned among us could see that he was right in quoting Deuteronomy and Leviticus. And the commandment to love others was a brilliant stoke of repartee. I even smiled when he said it.

But just as one of my colleagues was about to fire off another question to him, Jesus stared at me with a gaze that held me transfixed. And his voice surrounded me with the question of my lifetime: 'What do you think of the Christ?' he asked. 'Whose son is he?'

I quickly answered with the rote response of my tradition: 'The son of David.'

Just as quickly, Jesus countered with Psalm 110, saying 'If David calls Messiah Lord, then how is the Messiah his son?'

Suddenly, this vagabond was dangerous. And he was not dangerous because of who his disciples claimed him to be. To dwell on the issue of David and sonship is gravely to miss the point. The danger from Jesus came in his *first* question - 'What do you think of the Christ?'

It is not an overstatement to say that my world was shattered by that question. For all my life I professed to know, with some certainty, what I *did* think of the Christ.

As a child I learned that he was the Anointed One who would lead Israel out of bondage forever. To me, that meant that he would probably be a great military hero with battle prowess and obvious stature to command and lead forth the liberating troops of our people. The children in my village would play together, each of us taking turns being the Messiah, conquering enemies and liberating countless numbers.

As a youth, other images of Messiah began to take shape in my mind. For a while, I saw him not as a military hero but as a wandering healer, taking the sick in his hands and freeing them from their diseases; or as a sort of a magician who would offer fantastic powers to me in return for my allegiance.

As I grew to an adult and began to choose my profession, I remember thinking of Messiah as a great and powerful Judge, who had the wisdom to make right decisions to rule and govern our people with fairness and trust.

When Jesus asked me that question this morning - 'What do you think of the Christ?' - all of these images flashed before my mind. And, although I repeated the expected rote answer of my Pharisee brethren, I became aware that there have been even more messiahs than that for me, especially in recent years. They have demanded my attention, and called for my allegiance, each offering a promise of salvation in return.

For a long while, even back into my teen years, Popularity seemed the only Messiah I needed. I fought for it, conformed for it, denied my own needs and the needs of friends for it. Though I have seen clearly since then that such a messiah is short lived and empty, I must admit that I still crave the seeming acceptance it offers.

Similarly, the seductive messiahs of sexuality, money, and power sought my willing obedience. I confused the far off promises of the Anointed One with the present promises of things that made me feel good and look good to my friends. Again, I confess that, though I have enough experience to know their short lived emptiness, I still fall prey to their promises from time to time, showing them to be my messiah.

Finally, to acknowledge all of my behavioral answers to Jesus' question, I must add the messiahs of work and family to my lengthening list. To say that I worship at those two altars is drastically to understate the case. There is always more work to be done than I can accomplish in my ten hour days. Sometimes I bring work home and spend long hours poring over it, neglecting my body's need for rest and exercise; pushing aside the playful requests of family and friends, doting on the papers as though my salvation depended upon them.

And there is always more to be done with and for my family, my wife and two children, than I have resources to provide. I constantly feel alternately guilty and then angry about their demands on me and my demands on myself for them, acting, again, as though the fate of my soul depended on them.

'What do you think of the Christ?' he asked me. And all of those answers ran through my head. I guess I could say, in embarrassing honesty, that I believed what made me feel good was Christ, Messiah to me. And I suppose, if we're honest, most people do the same thing. We think that the Christ is the one who supports our political beliefs, our social understanding, the way we spend our money and our time. Instead of hearing and seeing the Messiah outside us, guiding, admonishing, correcting, supporting, accepting - we want the Christ to be made in our image.

Over the years, I became complacent and comfortable with my image of the Christ, not thinking much about it, letting those smaller messiahs I mentioned take its place. Until today. Until this Jesus person asked me that question.

It was as though he held up a mirror to my soul. I looked into that mirror and did not like what I saw. Because my answer to that question - What do you think of the Christ? - is reflected in everything else I do. It is shown in how I spend my money, what I do with my time, the words that come out of my mouth, what I say and think about other people who are different from me, how I treat strangers.

What I think of the Christ is obvious in my relationships with family and friends, in my behaviour at work and at home, by how I treat my co-workers, my children, my spouse. It is reflected in how I decide what is ethical when confronted with wrong or hurtful ideas. It is shown in how I take care of my body, what I put in my mouth to eat smoke chew or drink.

Perhaps most importantly, what I think of the Christ is reflected in who I love and how I love; in whether and how I am willing to forgive others, in whether or not I am willing to accept God's forgiveness and go on.

My quick answer to his question was an attempt to stop him, to make him put the mirror to my soul aside, to stop confronting me with the truth of my behaviour. But he was not finished with me yet.

My answer to his question was the old, familiar, safe answer - the son of David. It was what everyone else would have said, and it was what I believed, or so I thought until I heard Jesus' response. Because what he said to me was this: Whatever you think of the Christ - he is different from the way you see him. Beware of your pious certainty, and your adamant demand that everyone else, the messiah included, conform to your hardened image of him — or her.

For perhaps the Christ will be a woman, or speak a foreign tongue and be a different colour; perhaps the Christ will be poor and illiterate, or deformed or retarded.

Once again, the certainty of my life was shaken by this Jesus. No wonder he is both shunned and sought after, loved and hated, welcomed and rejected. He held up a mirror to my soul and, as if that was not enough, he shattered the comfortable image of the Christ that had been the basis of my belief all this time.

I walked away from him stunned. Nobody was able to ask him any more questions - or wanted to, for that matter. We learned that this Jesus is not a passive weakling. We learned that when you ask questions of him you had better be prepared to have him ask questions of you; uncomfortable, shattering, soul searching questions that could change your life.

I must bring this confession to a close by finally confessing that, although I would like to follow him, I cannot. My tradition is too strong, my previous beliefs too ingrained, my position in the community too established. And yet - I will never be the same. I am unable to see things the way I did before. It is as though this Jesus, by his simple question, brought my world into a different focus, demanded I see myself and my beliefs for what they really were, offered me another, freer image to follow.

I only wish that I could.

I don't know why I am writing this. No one else will ever read it. But if they do, I hope they, too, will let this Jesus hold a mirror up to their soul, and be confronted by his life changing answers about the Christ that they think they know so well, yet, like myself, may not know at all.

Unlike myself, perhaps they will be willing and able to follow him.

Mark 12.38-44

Teaching in the temple Jesus said, "Beware of the scribes, who like to go about in long robes, and to have salutations in the market places and the best seats in the synagogues and the places of honor at feasts, who devour widows' houses and for a pretense make long prayers. They will receive the greater condemnation."

And he sat down opposite the treasury, and watched the multitude putting money into the treasury. Many rich people put in large sums. And a poor widow came, and put in two copper coins, which make a penny. And he called his disciples to him, and said to them, "Truly, I say to you, this poor widow has put in more than all those who are contributing to the treasury. For they all contributed out of their abundance but she out of her poverty has put in everything she had, her whole living."

The Widow's Story

The sunlight softly nudged the chill of the morning from the room where the widow slept. She slowly opened her heavy lidded eyes, blinked them, then closed them again. Her first thought was the same as always.

It was another day without him.

But, she remembered, as she dragged herself up from the comfortable abyss of sleep, it was no ordinary day. It was, she painfully reminded herself, the twelfth anniversary of her husband's death.

Twelve years, she thought. Twelve years. Twelve years of this empty space beside her every morning. Twelve years of listening for, yearning for but never hearing his deep, reassuring voice calling her name. Twelve years of being alone, not always lonely, but always ultimately alone.

She rose from the bed and wandered to the basin of water she had set out the night before. She looked into the fragment of polished metal she used as a mirror, and saw the lines that agony and poverty had etched into her sagging skin. She had once been such a beautiful woman. That was what had attracted him in the first place. She smiled as she remembered their early days together.

Now, she told herself, she was old. She was very old. And today, after twelve years without him, she felt every day of her age.

She dressed quickly and pulled a chair up to the broken wooden table next to the bed. Her one room was small, but she had done what she could to make it comfortable. Her husband had had no brothers to care for her, so she had relied mainly on the generosity of others, and had occasionally been able to find odd work here and there. Recently, for almost a year she had worked as a maid in the house of a wealthy merchant, raising his children, cooking his meals, cleaning his clothes. But he soon remarried and moved away, and no longer needed her.

She had diligently saved the small amount of money she earned from that job, and had spent it sparingly, mainly on food, though some of it she had given at the temple.

The widow pulled together some scraps of food she had been given the day before. The hardened bread hurt her tender gums, until she dipped it in the cup of water from her neighbor's well. The fruit she had found in a meadow near the town. It was on the ground, and beginning to rot, but it would provide some sustenance for one more day, as would the small bit of meal she had made from the grains gleaned from the recent harvest.

She was grateful for her health, she mused, and she was grateful for her friends. The Master of the Universe had surely looked after her needs, and, even though she had no children, her life was not as barren as it looked to others.

Except, perhaps, for today. After twelve years.

She put the bread down and glanced toward the braided slats that served as a door. How could she still miss him, she wondered? How, after all this time, could she still want him to come through that door full of stories and anger and passion and hunger - and life? He was always, even into his later years, so full of life. Does desire never wane, she wondered?

She stood and went to the trunk where she kept her clothes. She opened the old, leather lid and reached down to the bottom underneath everything else. She pulled out a bundle of cloth tied with a string and set it on the table. Slowly, reverently, she untied the bundle and opened the cloth.

She smiled at herself as she looked at the well worn, ragged pair of sandals before her. She felt so silly. How could she have kept them all these years? She shook her head. What could they possibly mean now? And yet, she thought, and yet they were her only tangible memory of him.

She ran her hands gently over the rough, torn leather, now become brittle with age and disuse, and her memories, years of memories, were strong again.

Moments later, or was it more time than that, she dried her eyes and carefully wrapped the sandals again and set them on the bed. She would spend some time later cleaning out that trunk and replace the bundle then. For now, she thought, as she stood and took a deep breath, she must make the trip to the temple.

The widow finished the cup of water and drank one more. It would be a long walk to the temple in the morning heat, and she would need all her strength. She noted that, over the last few weeks, the walk seemed to be getting harder for her. She had to pause and rest more often, she was out of breath sooner walking up the small hills. Sometimes, she would have fits of coughing that made her feel nearly like she would never stop, or never get enough air in her lungs. Once, it had been just last Sabbath, she had passed out from one of those spells, and had had to be placed on a bench until she recovered.

The old woman started out the door, then stopped. She walked back to a small box beside the water basin and looked inside. There were only two copper coins left. She hesitated a moment, started to put the lid back on, then sighed as though coming to her senses, and put the two coins in her dress pocket.

The trip to the temple was as she expected. The sun was already high in the sky, beating its summer rays down on buildings, animals and people. The dust in the road seemed particularly bothersome to her, as she coughed more than usual. She found herself stopping often to catch her breath, and she counted herself blessed to have found a sturdy walking stick someone had abandoned on a side street.

After what seemed double the time it used to take, the widow saw the temple in the distance. She thought her fading eyesight must be playing tricks on her again, as there were large crowds around the building. She paused for a moment, pursed her dry lips and frowned, as though trying to get her head to remember the obvious.

No, she thought, it was not the Sabbath. And even then, these crowds do not appear except on high holy days. Maybe she should not venture into that throng, she worried. What if she had another spell? What if the heat overcame her? What if... Disappointed as she was, she decided not to risk it. She could pray to God in her own home. She could say the ritual as well as the priest in her own small room. She could...

As she turned to go back, the two coins in her pocket jingled as they touched each other. She stopped.

Twelve years, she thought. The Master of the Universe has sustained me for twelve years. I want to go and offer thanks, for my husband and his spirit and his memory, and to God for being with me.

The widow made her decision, and the coins jingled as she forced her heavy, tired legs back up the street to the temple steps. She concentrated on finding the shortest route through the crowd into the temple and so, in her distraction, did not acknowledge the scribes when she passed them. She cowered when she heard a rough voice yell at her in reprimand. She knew the scribes were men of power, and that they could wipe our her small one room home simply at whim if they chose. She vowed to be more attentive the next time.

Weaving her old frame through the tightly packed crowd was painful. The widow could hardly breathe by the time she reached the door at the back of the temple. She leaned against the wall for a moment to catch her breath and to get control, once again, of the coughing fit she thought was about to overtake her.

As she rested, her eyes fell on the young man standing on a bench over on the other side of the temple, near the treasury. He was talking to a large group of people, who seemed quite interested in all he had to say. She shrugged her shoulders, took a deep breath and shook her head. Another prophet, she thought. There were so many of them these days. All claiming special knowledge of God, all claiming special insight into Torah, all ending up with the money the temple had allotted for other things.

The widow made her way to an abandoned side pew on the opposite corner from where the man was speaking. She bowed her head and recited her prayers as she had done for decades. She became oblivious to the noisy crowd, focusing only on her reason for being there. And yet, and yet she seemed somehow drawn to that voice. She could barely hear his words, but the voice, the sound of it seemed to comfort her, even though it distracted her from her inner dialogue with God.

She finished her first set of ritual prayers and sat back to rest. It was such a long trek home, she would sit here, continuing to pray, for her friends, for the sick, for those less fortunate than she, for peace in this uncertain world, for children, for this young man whose voice had that special quality...and, for her husband, for his memory, for his life with her, for her life without him now.

The widow sat in the hard wooden seat for some time before the sound of the young man's voice again touched her and made the connection. She was at the end of her prayers when a certain word, a unique inflection struck her ear as clearly as someone tapping her on the shoulder. She turned around to look closer at this man - and she made the connection. That voice, so strong, so powerful, so confronting and comforting - this young man sounded much like her husband had in his early years.

She pushed her bulk up from the pew and stood, steadying herself on her slightly numb legs. Again she stifled a cough as she forced her way through the tangled mass of people toward the treasury. She would put her two meager coins in the plate. She would be laughed at by those putting in so much more. She would feel embarrassed, as always, that she did not have more to give, and feel bad that God had given her so much and she could return so little.

The coins jingled in her pocket. They were the last money she had, but this day, this twelve year day, she felt so full of emotion and gratefulness, that she had to give it all. And today, as if in return for her plan, she would hear up close the voice of this prophet, the voice that sounded so tender and familiar, the voice that reminded her of her husband.

She stood in the line that filed by the treasury, and, when her turn came, she averted her eyes from all those watching and dropped her two copper coins, one at a time, into the plate.

Muffled sounds came from the well dressed people standing by, until, suddenly, that voice silenced them all. It was as though time stood still for her. The prophet's voice took charge, and the widow slowly, fearfully looked up at him. Would he ridicule her also? Would he single her out for special condemnation?

Her already shaky legs felt weaker and she leaned more heavily on the walking stick.

She did not hear all of his words, he spoke so quickly to the crowd. But she did hear his voice, and look into his eyes. His was not the gaze of condemnation, nor the voice of ridicule. His voice surrounded her, calmed and comforted her, steadied her legs and strengthened her spirit. His eyes looked deep within her, seemed to know her through and through, loved her not with pity but with affirmation and acceptance.

Others from behind pushed her to move on. Before she averted her eyes from him she smiled at him, and his smile caused her eyes to well up and gently overflow.

The widow followed the line outside the temple and made her way down the steps to the dusty street again. She stifled a cough, then, when she could hold it no longer, she racked her body with spasms from her searing lungs. At last the fit stopped, and she rested a moment against a chipped plaster wall. When she recovered her strength, she walked, now with a different kind of step, down the hill on her long journey back home. Her mind whirled with thoughts that disregarded her illness and the hot sun: the prayers in the temple, the ridicule from the people, the prophet's voice and his words to them.

What was it he said? She could only remember bits of it. Something about giving all she had. How had he known that? And what did it mean?

She did not understand his words to the crowd, but she did understand his voice and his eyes, and his smile. Though her body ached and her lungs gasped for short breaths as she struggled toward home, inside she felt a calm she had not felt in a long, long time. For twelve years, she thought. Twelve years.

The widow entered her one room and, leaning heavily now on the walking stick, shakily lowered herself onto the bed. When she caught her heaving breath, she poured a small glass of water and sipped it, slowly, ever so slowly, trying to calm her agitated body and give it rest.

After a while, her heart stopped racing and her legs relaxed. Even her lungs seemed to take their shallow breaths more easily. She drank the rest of the water and, feeling tired from her extraordinary morning, swung her throbbing legs up on the bed and laid her head back on the lumpy straw pillow.

Her thoughts drifted back to the way she had awakened, as she closed her tired eyes and recounted the events of the day. Twelve years, she thought. Twelve years.

Her breathing became more shallow still, as her mind fell deeper, deeper into a place far away from the present. The prophet's voice calmed her, welcomed her, comforted her. What was it he had said? Maybe now she could remember. Something about giving up everything. Something about giving all they had.

An inner smile warmed her. She had nothing now. And she suddenly had everything. Is that what he meant? When we truly give it all up, our fears, our guilt, our poverty, our riches, our love, our anxiety, our embarrassment - then we get abundance back?

She wondered how the young man knew all this, and what he would do when he was in the same situation. He would probably trust the Master of the Universe, Adonai; he would probably take the same risk, for how could he not do so? He had been given so much, just as she had. He had been given that voice, those eyes, those words, that smile.

The widow felt her lungs tightening within her. She put her right hand on her chest, where the heavy pressure seemed to be. But she was not afraid. It was a passing spasm, just as before. Her breaths became more and more shallow as she fell deeper and deeper into a comfortable darkness lighted only by the voice of that prophet...or was it now the voice of her husband?

At last, she took a deep breath; she sighed a sigh that ended pain, ended suffering, relieved her from the burden of her aching spent form, released her into that voice of light that welcomed and rested and healed.

And, as she did, her left hand fell upon the small bundle of cloth, tied with a string, the bundle she had not yet put away.

At that same moment, in the temple, Jesus stopped in the middle of a sentence. He looked at the crowd clamoring around him. He glanced around at his puzzled disciples.

Then, suddenly, he left the temple. And he spoke no more that day.

References

Genesis 1.1-2, 2.................1

Exodus 16.2-4, 9-15 80

Proverbs 9.1-16 96

Zechariah 9.9-12 73

Matthew 22.35-40 153

Mark 2.1-12 10

Mark 4.35-41, 5.1-2 123

Mark 6.30-34 26

Mark 6.45-52 62

Mark 11.1-11 ....34, 107

Mark 12.38-44 162

Luke 4.1-13 53

Luke 7.11-17 146

Luke 9.18-24 42

Luke 17.11-19 135

John 2.1-11..............48

John 6.3-15...............17

Acts 9.1-19a..............86

Acts 16.16-34............116

Books by Chuck Meyer

Surviving Death: A Practical Guide to Caring for the Dying and Bereaved. 23rd Publications, Mystic, Connecticut, 1988, Second Edition, 1991. ($9.95) - This book is for those who care for the dying, the families and friends of the terminally ill, those who have experienced the death of a close loved one, and those who themselves are dying. Dr. Karl Slaikeu, author of Up From The Ashes says: "...the book is unsurpassed in its concrete, step-by-step instructions on everything from walking into the patient's room, to talking with dying and bereaved individuals and coping with the full range of emotions and behavioral demands that survivors face. The author's blend of humor and sensitivity is especially refreshing." Winner of the Violet Crown Award for best non-fiction book of 1991, Austin Writer's League. (175pp.)

God's Laughter and Other Heresies. Stone Angel Books, Austin, Texas, Second Edition 1992. ($9.95). The author guarantees that "the buying of this book will definitely increase your own personal chances of getting into heaven." If heaven is a place of joy, sadness, tears and laughter, then he is correct, for the book is filled with all of the above. In addition to the slightly irreverent commentaries on "Babies," "Stress," and "Bible Misquotes," the Christmas stories of "A Donkey Named Glory," "The Fourth Wise Man," "Harold the Innkeeper," and "An Angel Named Bubba," make delightful reading to children. (238pp.)

The Eighth Day, Letters, Poems and Parables. Stone Angel Books, Austin, Texas 1991. ($8.95). The Eighth Day is the day after God finished making everything and rested. It is the time *after* the seventh day and *before* Jesus comes back. It is sort of a Christian Twilight Zone where the Holy Spirit plays Rod Serling. These "letters, poems and parables" retell Bible stories from the viewpoint of the characters themselves. The Widow's Story, The Lawyer's Confession, Three Days in Saul's Head, Leper Letter, and The Paralytic's Point of View, vividly portray the feelings and thoughts of ordinary people encountering an ordinary Jesus with extraordinary results for the rest of their lives. (175pp.)

The Gospel According to Bubba. Stone Angel Books, Austin, Texas, 1992. ($9.95). A 250lb Texas angel named Bubba appeared at the author's front door with "inside" information from "The Boss" and one heck of a thirst. It was down hill from there. Bubba's (unsolicited) insights are as Lone Star as "fahr aints." He's got comments on everything from Genesis to Bethlehem, from Blue Bell to Shiner Bock. If you're a Texan (native or born again) you'll cotton to stories like Beach Blanket Bubba, Bubba at Deep Eddy, and Bubba at Dime Box - and you'll want to share him with your friends. (176pp.)

Books may be purchased at your local bookstore or by using this form:

Stone Angel Books
P O Box 27392
Austin, Texas 78755-2392

Please send:

___ *Surviving Death* ($9.95) $ _____

___ *God's Laughter* ($9.95)   _____

___ *The Eighth Day* ($8.95)   _____

___ *Gospel/Bubba* ($9.95)   _____

Texans (excluding Bubba) add 8% tax   _____

Postage/handling
    1 book/$1.25   _____
    2 books/$2.00   _____
    3 books/$3.00   _____
    4 books/FREE   _____

TOTAL $ _____

Make check or Money Order payable to

Stone Angel Books

Name _____

Address _____

City _____ State _____ Zip _____

(Want books autographed? Indicate "to whom".)